Lolas' House

M. Evelina Galang

Lolas' House

Filipino Women
Living with War

CURBSTONE BOOKS / NORTHWESTERN UNIVERSITY PRESS
EVANSTON, ILLINOIS

Curbstone Books
Northwestern University Press
www.nupress.northwestern.edu

FRONTISPIECE: Lolas of LILA Pilipina protest in front of the Japanese
embassy in Manila, July 9, 2002.

Printed in the United States of America

10   9   8   7   6   5   4   3   2   1

Library of Congress Cataloging-in-Publication Data

Names: Galang, M. Evelina, 1961– author.
Title: Lolas' House : Filipino women living with war / M. Evelina Galang.
Description: Evanston, Illinois : Curbstone Books / Northwestern University
    Press, 2017.
Identifiers: LCCN 2017013878 | ISBN 9780810135864 (pbk. : alk. paper) |
    ISBN 9780810135871 (e-book)
Subjects: LCSH: Comfort women—Philippines. | World War, 1939–1945—
    Personal narratives, Philippine. | World War, 1939–1945—Women—
    Philippines. | World War, 1939–1945—Atrocities—Philippines.
Classification: LCC D810.C698 .G35 2017 | DDC 940.5308209599—dc23
LC record available at https://lccn.loc.gov/2017013878

LABAN mga Lola! LABAN! LABAN! LABAN!

For the women of Liga ng mga Lolang Pilipina—
may you see the light of justice.

My mother washed my back as if I had left for only a day and were her baby yet. "We are going to carve revenge on your back," my father said. "We'll write out oaths and names."

—Maxine Hong Kingston, *The Woman Warrior*

CONTENTS

Welcome to Lolas' House   6

Through the Mercy of God   13
    Catalina Lorenzo   16
    Virginia Villarma   30
    Lucia Alvarez   36
    Pilar Frias   54

"Turtle! Turtle!"   65
    Benita Aliganza   68
    Cristita Alcober   80
    Narcisa Adriatico Claveria   100
    Violeta Lanzarote   116

They Used Us   123
    Prescila Bartonico   126
    Dolores Pasarang Molina   136
    Piedad Nicasio Nobleza   150
    Josefa Lopez Villamar   158

Japanese Leftovers   177
    Atanacia Cortez   180
    Urduja Samonte   200
    Carmencita Cosio Ramel   216
    Remedios Felias   226

Justice by Knife   233
    Filipino "Comfort Women" of World War II   248

Monday's Luminous Mysteries: An Afterword   255

Acknowledgments   261

400,000   265

Further Reading   267

Welcome to Lolas' House

Navotas, Metro Manila

THE FIFTEEN-PASSENGER van climbs up the mountain passage, rising above Metro Manila. Below, mismatched rooftops, jagged and rusty, roll across the city. Houses scatter like toys spilling everywhere. Smog sits like a bad hat, odd shaped and heavy atop the skyscraping towers. The city has gone on strike and basurero have left garbage on the roadsides to rot. We can smell it even after we've raised the windows and cranked the air conditioner. The older girls are wide-eyed, heads pressed against the windows, necks stretching to see the makeshift plywood shanties, where doors are old bedsheets and laundry is hung to dry like fences between neighbors. Now and then a curtain slips open and a handful of schoolchildren march out in plaid skirts and sailor tops, in long pants and short-sleeved button-down shirts and backpacks too big for their bodies. The children go to school in shifts.

Inside the van our driver cranks Manila pop radio, a clutter of singsong jingles, cloying announcers, and loud radio banter. Nobody sounds real. Everyone is happy. The whole van pulses a bad disco beat, grinding its way uphill. We drive past a naked child bathing in a rubber tire, his grandmother squatted to the road and soaping him down, his mouth wide open and howling. The two teens with us, Eliza and Lizzie, have headphones on and are singing to each other in the way-back seat. In the middle row, Ana Fe and Tara sit at opposite windows while Neleh, poised in between, bops up and down to the radio as always, as if she has lived here all her life. As we pass the naked child and his lola,

3

Ana Fe jabs Neleh; pointing to the kid in the squalor of garbage, she says, "Slap me upside the head if I ever complain again."

FORTY-EIGHT HOURS earlier, we six Filipino American girls, with enough luggage for a dozen people, landed on the tarmac at Manila International, drove through the sleeping streets of the metropolis, through the back alleys of Malate. We pulled up to the gates of Nursia, a dormitory for the Institute of Women's Studies at St. Scholastica's College. We had been on the road for more than twenty-four hours and we were slaphappy, glad to be "back home." When we rang Nursia's bell, a security guard with a long gun opened the gate. His jaw square, locked, his eyes unblinking. Everyone was asleep. No one to be found at the front desk. Just a sign on a giant whiteboard that read, "Six guests from America arrive tomorrow."

Now we are traveling to the Navotas meeting of Liga ng mga Lolang Pilipina, a.k.a. LILA Pilipina, the league of Filipina grandmothers, and I can feel the anticipation of two years of research rising up in me, a hum in the back of my throat growing louder and louder and I know we're close. Until this moment, all I had found were a smattering of facts from one text, a handful of reports from the MacArthur Memorial archives, and one slim book about Korean "comfort women" from the Washington Coalition for Comfort Women Issues. I wanted to meet a survivor. I wanted to see her face and to know her stories. Just before our trip had been finalized in 1997, I received Lola Maria Rosa Henson's autobiography, *Comfort Woman, Slave of Destiny*. She was the first Filipina "comfort woman" to come forward publicly. I thought I would meet her, but she died of a heart attack in August 1997. But now, the faces. Now, the women. We're almost there. And I wonder, what are they going to be like?

The van rolls to a stop in front of a house on a dirt road. People stream out onto the porch. Children and elders and little brown women.

"This is it," Tara says as she shuts her eight-week itinerary and shoves it into her backpack.

"Here we go," I say.

Lolas' House, 49 Matimpiin Street, Central District, Quezon City
June 1999

WELCOME to Lolas' House

FILIPINA "COMFORT WOMEN" were among the women and girls systematically abducted by the Imperial Japanese Army during World War II and forced into military rape camps all over Asia. Women were similarly taken in China, Korea, Dutch Indonesia, Malaysia, Australia, New Zealand, and Japan. Early research by the scholars Margaret Stetz and Bonnie Oh suggests there were anywhere from 50,000 to 200,000 women abducted. But in a study published in 2013, Peipei Qiu included new estimates for Chinese "comfort women" that doubled the total estimate to 400,000. In the Philippines, the Japanese army coerced more than 1,000 Filipinas into sex slave camps. Of those women, 174 have come forward. I have had the honor of meeting 40 of them through LILA Pilipina and have interviewed 16 extensively for this book.

The existence of World War II–era "comfort women" in the Philippines was first brought to attention in December 1991, when a delegation from the Filipino chapter of the Asian Women's Human Rights Council (AWHRC) attended a regional conference in Seoul on the trafficking of women in Asia. Around the same time, in South Korea three women gained wide attention when they went public with their stories. At the conference, the Korean delegation announced that between 70,000 and 200,000 Korean women were coerced into sex slavery. Shortly thereafter, the *Philippine Daily Inquirer* reported that a Japanese medical document dated March 19, 1942, mentioned 19 Filipina "comfort women" from Iloilo, and gave a partial listing of 13 names. The report also included a sketch of a "comfort station" near the city plaza.

AWHRC and another nongovernmental organization, BAYAN–Women's Desk, called on Cory Aquino, then Philippine president, to investigate. Aquino's Presidential Commission on Human Rights charged Ricardo Jose, a professor at the University of the Philippines, to research and report on the issue. Jose submitted a report on June 26, 1992, concluding that no large-scale efforts at conscription took place.

Not satisfied with the Jose report, on July 13, 1992, AWHRC and BAYAN–Women's Desk, along with fourteen women's organizations including GABRIELA National Women's Coalition, created the Task Force on Filipino "Comfort Women." Eventually, the task force would be renamed Liga ng mga Lolang Pilipina, a.k.a. LILA Pilipina. Its mission was to research and coordinate legal matters, public information, and education for the various groups' efforts. A call went out to former Filipina "comfort women" to step forward. They set up hotlines and issued daily calls to action on the radio.

On September 18, 1992, Maria Rosa Henson, then sixty-five, became the first Filipina "comfort woman" to tell her story publicly. In her 1996 autobiography, *Comfort Woman: Slave of Destiny*, Lola Rosa says that one day, while hanging laundry, she heard a woman on the radio talking about girls who had been taken by the army. Until then, she had kept her past a secret from everyone except her mother. When Lola Rosa heard Liddy Alejandro of BAYAN–Women's Desk talk about the "comfort women," she had a visceral reaction, shaking and crying. She didn't respond to the call at first. In fact, she tried to forget it, but when she heard the announcement a second time, weeks later, she broke into tears again, and when her daughter heard her crying, she ran to her.

During my interviews with the women of LILA Pilipina, they would share their testimonies of abduction, but they would also talk about the moment Lola Rosa came forward. Her story led many of the women to tell their stories—173 followed her example.

By April 2, 1993, eighteen Filipinas along with task force coordinators Nelia Sancho and Indai Sajor filed a lawsuit at the Tokyo District Court of Japan. Twenty-eight women joined the lawsuit in September of that year. Their demands were simple. They wanted

(1) a formal apology,

(2) compensation for their suffering, and

(3) documentation in official histories.

Japanese courts denied the lawsuit, though several appeals were made. The women have yet to receive anything—no formal apology from the government, no compensation, and no definitive place in history.

Most of the Filipinas who survived sex slavery by the Imperial Japanese Army went on to live full lives. Some married and bore many children. Others became vendors in the market or washerwomen or maids, wives of mayors, or classroom teachers. Still, there were the ones who would go mad and never recover. By the time the women began their campaign for justice, they had grown so old that the people called them "lolas," the Tagalog word for "grannies."

I FIRST MET the women while I was researching a screenplay called *Dalaga*, the Tagalog word for that in-between moment when a girl is no longer a girl and yet not quite a woman. The movie was going to explore the relationship between a Filipina American dalaga and her lola—a grandmother who also happened to be a surviving "comfort woman." I wanted to know what the lola could teach the dalaga about being a woman. So during summer 1998, I traveled with five Filipina American dalagas to meet the women of LILA Pilipina.

We met the survivors at Lolas' House, the offices of LILA Pilipina, a bungalow set in the middle of Metro Manila's Quezon City. Here, organizers held general assemblies year round. In addition to their campaign for justice, the lolas planned upcoming activities and other strategic events, and, most important, bonded with one another and their supporters. Organizers from LILA Pilipina also would travel to the women's communities—Antipolo, Navotas, and Manila (the "Mix-Mix" group)—to meet with smaller gatherings of women.

For eight weeks, my charges and I met every day with the lolas, acting, drawing, writing letters, and protesting in front of the Japanese and American embassies, raising our fists at the gates of Malacañang Palace. During these activities the lolas of LILA Pilipina came to know the dalagas—twenty-somethings Tara Agtarap, Ana Fe Muñoz, and Neleh Barcarse, and teenagers Lizzie Juaniza and Eliza Habón. As our friendships grew, the stories burst forth like water from a dam. Horrific testimonies of habitual rape and torture.

At the end of those eight weeks, the women at Lolas' House surrounded me. Most of them came to the middle of my chest. They stood on their toes to sniff my face. They refused to say goodbye. Instead, they asked, "When are you coming back?" "When are you going to write our stories?" They didn't want a screenplay—not a movie, not even a book of fiction. They wanted to document their stories and they asked me to do it.

I RETURNED ON a Fulbright from 2001 to 2002.

I knocked on the thick green gate and listened. A videoke machine thumped through the concrete walls and I heard the lolas' voices humming like bees just underneath the music. The gate creaked open and I left the broken streets of Matimpiin, the rubble at the curb, and the overgrown green weeds, and I stepped onto the patio at Lolas' House. Their faces turned to the door. I smiled. Yelled, "Kamusta, Lola?" Rechilda "Ritchie" Extremadura, the executive director of LILA Pilipina, looked away from the TV screen for a moment, microphone in hand. "Ito na," she told the lolas, announcing my arrival. Then she continued singing. The lolas had been waiting since early morning and they were randomly scattered across the patio. When they realized it was me stepping through the gate, they let out sighs and called my name. Some of them scolded me for making them wait. They wanted to know if I had eaten. As I walked through the patio, they rose to greet me, each one holding onto a part of me. Their voices grew louder than the videoke and they swarmed about me, pulling at my fingers, holding my hands, or rubbing my back. Several sets of thin arms wrapped around my waist. I felt the light kisses on my shoulders and arms. I felt the bony fingers pinching at my skin. I kissed each one of them, looking them in the eye, and each one held my face in her small hands for just a second before letting go and stepping away.

DURING MY FULBRIGHT research, I traveled with seven lolas, taking each one to the different islands and provinces of the Philippine archipelago where they were abducted and imprisoned—to abandoned churches, city halls, farmhouses, and schools. Survivors took me to sites where their grass-roofed houses used to stand, and together we relived their experiences.

I stood quietly in each space and closed my eyes. I considered the lives that were damaged there and I saw ghosts of soldiers walking with their guns and bayonets held up. I heard the crying of girls left swollen and bleeding, only to be taken once more without a moment to clean themselves. Somehow in those moments I became one of those girls. The land, which was part of my ancestry, felt like home. The strength of the women reminded me of the strength of the women in my family.

WE SPOKE IN half sentences. I had a habit of speaking Tagalog backward. I transposed letters and reduced the words to meaningless utterings. I left words out. I created new ones. But we understood each other anyway.

At first, the organizers of LILA would translate the lolas' words, then I used a translator until I understood Tagalog better than I could speak it. When I realized the translator could not transpose the emotional content of the conversation, I let him go. I relied on the lola's voice, her facial expressions, and her body language. I took my cues from the way she reacted to me and my questions. The lolas and I began developing our own mix of Tagalog and English. At the end of a sixteen-hour day, sitting in the stalled heat of Manila traffic, my driver, Faustino Bong Cardiño, also engrossed in the lolas' stories, would unpack the day's events with me.

Since 1998, I have taped more than forty hours of interviews. I have visited at least seven sites of abduction and former "comfort stations." There are binders of transcriptions and translations of the conversations I have held with the sixteen women in this book. A tribe of translators has taken down their words and given them English meaning. I cleaned up the sentences and streamlined the stories, but in the end, I felt it was important for each lola to testify for herself. So the abduction testimonies are written in their own words.

These stories, these kwentos, are a gift that I have received, and as I pass them on, part of the story is the way they came to me. Because I am American born, because my cultural understanding of being Filipina has been handed down to me in a Midwestern, first-world upbringing, the stories arrived in bits and pieces. Sometimes the lolas, the organizers, and I experienced roadblocks of understanding. I'd ask a question and the lola would ignore it and speak her mind. Sometimes our definitions of activism took on the form of writing, poetry, and drawing, and sometimes it meant marching in the streets. Oftentimes we had to speak the stories, hear the stories, repeat them in more than one language to arrive at our destination, the page. When it was possible, the lola gave me her testimony more than once—once in 1998, once in 2001, and then again when I could find written testimony given to other reporters or the Japanese lawyers who defended them in Tokyo. In their investigation of the lolas' cases, Japanese lawyers sought witnesses to corroborate each woman's claim. When I asked for these versions of the testimonies, the organization hesitated to give them to me. We went back and forth before the pages were released. I used the various pieces of evidence as a way to verify the testimonies I received. I interviewed them on more than one occasion in order to make sure I had understood the story they were telling.

The text that follows is in English, but it is seasoned with words handed down to me by the lolas. Some cannot be translated. What I can convey is the emotional charge they carry. Tagalog words and phrases are set in context, and you can derive their meaning by the way the lola, the organizer, and I act and interact, for these are the ways I also came to understand the lolas' plight. Often words will become clear to readers later in the text.

Mostly, the experience of recording these testimonies was visceral. My Tagalog eventually straightened itself out and their English found meaning, but in the beginning we spoke with our hands. The kwentos of the lolas were written on the spines of their backs. Often, they guided my fingers to their wounds. I read them, slowly, tentatively, my touch light and respectful. Unlike broken sentences of English and Tagalog and Waray, the scars needed no translation.

I set my hand at the base of an old woman's spine, or in the hollow between her breasts, or in the meat of her calf. The tips of my fingers examined the shape of the scar, the size of a bump, its density. A cigarette burn. A bayonet wound. A crooked finger. My skin absorbed the memory and I whispered, "Yes, Lola. I know, Lola." Together we searched for her lost voice. Was it here in her chest, was it embedded in the thigh, was it stuck in the throat or weighed down in the belly? We strained to hear and we were hoping to set that calamity free, to stop it from happening again.

I made a promise to the lolas. I told them I would write their stories. I told them I would document their experiences so that the world would have a record of what happened, so that we would have an understanding of what happens to women in war. Every time a woman speaks her testimony, she relives that moment when she was kidnapped, those days and weeks when she was held captive and repeatedly raped. You might think it would be easier to stay quiet. But holding onto these stories proved more painful. These women believed telling their stories would keep their daughters and granddaughters safe. They had faith that their fight for just compensation, an apology, and documentation in history books would keep this story from happening again.

That apology has yet to come. Government compensation to all "comfort women" has not been paid. And perhaps worst of all, the Japanese government has done its best to erase the women from our communal memory. Such stories repeat themselves even today. See it in Bosnia. See it in Syria. See it in the Congo.

What follows is a collection of testimonies told to me by the women themselves. It is their offering to us all. It is the promise that I made. I am the first American-born Filipina in a large family; I am a sister, an auntie, a stepmother, a wife. I recently become a lola. I am a professor who mentors many young women. Writing this book, I could not help but think of all my girls. My brothers' daughters are dalagitas now—twelve and fourteen and seventeen years old—the same age as the lolas when they were taken hostage.

NOW THE LOLAS' kwentos buzz like bees in my ear. Swarming, they sting me. They manifest in a migraine, in a backache, in the inability to sleep. They fly right down the length of both my legs, their needles pricking me as they go. I feel them hovering at the soles of my feet, and there is a tenderness that swells. I know I cannot rest until the stories are told. Until the apology is made. Until a woman's body is no longer desecrated in war and all the lolas regain their dignity.

Through the Mercy of God

IN OUR MOST intimate conversations, you will hear the lolas say Sa awa ng Diyos. Like a chorus to a song, or the last prayer on a string of beads. Sa awa ng Diyos.

After fifty years, the women come forward. One by one, they hear the story of Lola Rosa Henson on the radio—a woman like themselves, shamed into silence. But not anymore. Is there anybody else, she wants to know. Are there others?

And one at a time, the women take a jeepney to Lolas' House. They ask their grandchildren to bring them. They ride a motor tricycle with their grown daughters. A former beauty queen greets them, helps them organize, tells them to fight. For the first time, the grannies will sit together and see women who have had to endure the same secret for fifty years. They will speak their stories. They will stand on streets in protest. They will seek justice.

How did you manage it, you ask. How? You say, Paano, Lola? Paano?

And they look at you and smile. Sa awa ng Diyos, they whisper. Through the mercy of God. It doesn't matter if she is Catholic, or Muslim, or if God has not seen the walls of her kitchen; she will at some point tell you, I have made it through the mercy of God.

Sa awa ng Diyos.

CATALINA LORENZO

Born December 24, 1914,
Tondo City, Metro Manila

Abducted by the Imperial
Japanese Army, 1942,
Davao City, Mindanao

Filed Postwar Compensation
Suit, September 1993,
Tokyo District Court

The flight of Lola Catalina Lorenzo

THE DALAGAS AND I sit among a circle of forty lolas in a half-built house of concrete blocks with smooth cement floors, waiting. Eliza and Lizzie sit next to one another, leaning their teen bodies one into the other like vines of sampaguita flowers, sleepy and green on a hot summer afternoon. Tara sits next to me—alert and ready to go with notebook on her lap, pen poised. On the other side of the circle, Neleh has already begun making friends with a few of the lolas and I can see her teasing them and laughing. Meanwhile, Ana Fe has taken out her video camera and begun shooting everything. I am seated and watch everything unfold. I carry with me the posture of the teacher. Eighty-five-year-old Lola Catalina Lorenzo leans back in her plastic chair and smiles at everyone sweetly. Her black eyes are magnified in the lenses of her glasses. She has dyed her hair pitch black and pulled it away from her face so it appears clean and soft and cradled in wrinkles. She seems indifferent to the chatter. She's perched at the very edge of the circle, and her eyes dart back and forth, following the other women's words. Each one speaks a little louder than the last.

"Taga saan sila?" one of the women wants to know.

"Taga America sila," answers Gema, one of the organizers.

"Tangkad naman," another woman remarks. So tall.

"Kano?" American?

17

They're talking about us like we cannot hear them. Oh, I hear them. And every word I translate in my head from Tagalog to English back to Tagalog. The process slows me down. In a few weeks, I'll hear them and know. The words will sink into my skin and I will know. But for now, this.

At five feet nine inches, I am the tallest woman in the room, so tall that the Filipinas think one of my parents must be "American," and by that they mean white. It takes me a moment to translate the phrases back to Tagalog. My blood—dugo ko—is purong Pilipino. Well, Filipino and Chinese, as many Filipinos are. My father is six feet tall, siya ay matangkad. He is the reason I tower over all the women.

The words come faster and I strain to keep up. Soon, each woman leaps into the conversation just as the other finishes. The gaps between their comments dissolve and they begin to speak over each other. Lola Catalina sits forward. She pulls her chair further into the circle. She leans on both elbows. One of the more dramatic ladies pounds on her chest. And without warning, Lola Catalina shoots her small body up out of her seat and shouts, "Filipinos did not fight in the war! The Filipinos were quiet. Tapos, the Americans came and made a playground out of the Philippines!"

Lola Catalina places her hands in prayer position before her heart, then sends them up like rockets. She whirls in circles before a window and the sun blazes behind her, erasing the expressions on her face. The light pushes through her floral skirt and I see her legs, bent and wiry. Her shadow darts about the room, circles fellow survivors, a few organizers, the five dalagas, and me. "It is as if they are slicing the sky," she says, now separating her long, thin arms as if there are shards of blue falling around her. I see a hand reach up to pull her down; someone attempts to pet her, to calm her, but she cannot stop now. "Ingat, Lola," calls out a voice, a warning. Everything she ever thought in these fifty years of silence unravels before us. "What do you think? We don't need their money, we need their sincere apology, we need justice. Americans and Japanese—did you see what they did to our country? To our women? To our families?"

Lola Catalina's accent reminds me of my elders when they are debating—old aunts and uncles, lolas and lolos, and our parents. I recognize the heat of the voice, understand the movement of the hands. I know once an idea finds its way inside them, like an ember from a hot flame, it ignites and burns at the flesh until tongues of fire lash out and take over the mind, the body, the soul. So when Lola Catalina stands before me in this way, pulsing each word and pointing at the end of each statement, I am taken home; I feel a sense of family and an impulse also to put my hand to the small of her back, to guide her gently to her seat.

Lola Catalina Lorenzo was born in Tondo, a district in Manila. Her father and my father come from Macabebe, Pampanga. She looks at me, shooting those words right at me. "Even if the whole world knows what they did to the Philippines, it will be very hard to make up for it. That's why, what you're doing, you'll never really know. But me, I am old. I know what they did here."

She says the war was between the Japanese and the Americans. The foreigners came and disrupted their lives, destroyed their city and all the Philippines. "It was their war," she yells, "and we were the ones who were victimized." She curls her sticklike fingers into fists, punching at the air. "Ang dugo nila," says one of the organizers, "Ay purong Pilipino. Ang magulang nila, taga dito." The organizers try to explain that even though we live in America, our blood is pure Pinay.

Lizzie and Eliza jump, pull away from each other, and sit, tall and big-eyed. Ana Fe has a lens to her eye and she is swish-panning her camera around the circle.

I fear Lola Catalina may collapse, that a heart hot with such passion might give out in a body so small and bones so frail. I want to tell her I, too, am Kapampangan. I can say *come here*—mekeni—and I can say *yes*—uwa. My last name means respect in Tagalog. I am the daughter of Miguel Trinidad Galang and the granddaughter of Miguel Galang Sr., who was a soldier in the Filipino army and a dentist who served all of Macabebe. The Galang house in Macabebe is across the street from the elementary school, the place the Japanese soldiers took and made into a garrison. I am the daughter of Gloria Anca Lopez-Tan, whose mother, Clara Anca, was the Filipina child bride of Philemon Green Lopez-Tan Siok Ching, a Chinese businessman who had relocated to Quezon Province. I have grown up in Wisconsin among the descendants of Germans and Poles, but I have been raised with the same values Lola Catalina's family instilled in her. More than anything, I want her to see me as I am and to trust me. But on this first day, in June 1999, her hands flutter fast like knives slicing the air, her voice begins down at the bottom of her feet and pushes up like a volcano, erupting, her words splattering the air.

At the moment Lola Catalina speaks and dive-bombs the air with her hands, my understanding of Tagalog is tattered and I catch the meaning of one out of every hundred words.

"Panay hearing-hearing."

The words come too fast.

Always hearings.

Too deep.

"Walang katarungan."

Too many.

No justice.

I hear one word I know and I must stop to translate it but by the time I do, she has spewed forth a thousand other words I do not know.

"Laging hearing-hearing." She swings her arms. "Walapang justice. Matanda na kami!"

She has gathered all her strength, all her years of suffering, of nightmares, of shame, and she is tossing it at us—*Always hearings. Nothing but hearings. And no answer. No justice. Only more hearings. We are old. We are dying. Enough hearings. Answer us!* A thousand memories, a thousand broken promises, and they are hitting the walls, shattering at our feet. It is too dangerous for us to stand, to walk amid this rubble, to escape.

We have no other choice than to sit very still, to listen, to let her anger fill the room and break into a million pieces.

EIGHT WEEKS LATER, Lola Catalina volunteers to give me and Ana Fe her testimony, and I am excited and a little nervous. I cannot seem to let go of the image of Lola Catalina's waiflike shadow darting back and forth, her hands slashing each word with a gush of hot air, with the rise of a voice that cracks loud as thunder.

On the patio of Lolas' House, surrounded by all the other grannies who are sitting on plastic chairs, gossiping to one another, Lola Catalina sits before me. She sniffs my cheek. I lean over and hold her hand. Her skin falls away from her thin bones and warms mine. I watch the way the veins in her hand map little roadways. She speaks to me and not the camera:

My mister was the private of General Paulino Santos. That was his destiny. We were among the 3,000 Filipino settlers sent to Glan, Mindanao. We called the place Dadiangas because there was nothing on that land but rocks and cogongrass. We were first batchers, my mister and I. By 1942 we built a house made out of mountain trees. We had a seven-month-old son by then and while my mister worked, I stayed home to care for our boy.

We heard the Japanese landed in Manila so I already knew it was only time before they came. Most of the men joined the Filipino guerrillas or went into the mountains to hide. Then one day—yun na—tahimik ang mundo—quiet. Three Japanese carriers sailed into our harbor and shot their fighter pilots from the decks. Naku! The sound was loud—the bullets fell from the bellies of planes like thunder. When I heard the planes, I sent my mister and my son to the mountains. Later that day, some of the women and I were in the fields when the planes flew over-head. The Japanese could see everything from the sky—and there was no place to hide so we women had to run through the tall grass, hiding behind the smoke and fire, dodging bullets—maingay naman! So noisy! Natakot kami!

I ran through the smoke. I dodged flames on the cogongrass. Fire from the sky missed me. When I looked to the ground I could see the bullets cracking the earth. I ran, even though I was not sure where I was going. The thick smoke made breathing difficult.

After the planes flew off, I joined my mister on the mountain-side. He and my son were hiding in an abandoned carabao cart. Tapos, we placed a mat in the bottom of the cart and blankets of grass over our son. High up in the mountains, we thought we'd be able to see everything before the Japanese could do anything. There were a thousand families hiding in those moun-tains. When it was quiet again, my mister and my son came back to me.

Then one night, I was cooking when a guard from the bottom of the mountain began to shout. The Japanese were coming, they were coming. So I sent my mister off again. This time he wrapped a kerchief around our son's mouth to keep him quiet, and they hid in the bark of a rotting tree.

I did my best to remain calm as a Japanese captain and soldier approached. They had brown uniforms, with long flaps that covered their ears. The captain wore a saber that ran all the way down his legs.

"Kura! Kura!" they shouted. "Where is your mister?"

"I have no mister."

"Where is your mister?"

"Nothing. I have none. He already died."

"Where do you live?" they asked me.

"Here," I told them.

"You are lying. You have a mister. You hid him. Show us. Where is your mister?"

"Oh no. No mister. Only me."

"Good. If there's no mister, we'll take you. Tell us, where is your mister."

Lola Catalina doesn't tell me what happens before they put her into a garrison, or after she is locked up, or what they do to her. She goes to the end—the part all the lolas love to tell. And then the Americans came, and MacArthur came back like he said he would. When the Japanese general heard this, they gathered all their things and they escaped, leaving behind a room full of women, a room of Muslim Filipino prisoners, and, in a third room, Lola Catalina Lorenzo. She nods at me and says, "But you know before they left they used me again." Ginamit nila ako. *They used me.* The phrase is left open, wide like the doors after the Japanese escaped. *They used me.* The phrase sounds innocent, clean. When the lolas cannot say rape, or when they cannot talk about being thrown down and pried open, when the words may rekindle old pain, they say ginamit nila ako. *They used me.* Over and over again, she says, *they used me.*

As the Japanese soldiers left the house in Dadiangas, the Filipino guerrillas came out of hiding and released the prisoners. The guerrillas came, she tells me, and they opened the doors and let everyone free. They went into the wells and they pulled out the bodies of the dead and buried them properly. They ran after the Japanese, and any they found they killed on their way.

22

The guerrillas found me in the middle room and they took me to Doctor Patag. Ang sakit ang katawan ko! My body was so weak he kept me in the hospital for a month while the guerrillas went looking for my mister and son.

When they found my mister, they brought him and the boy before me. He looked at me for a long time and I waited for him to embrace me, but he did not.

"I thought you had died," he told me. I shook my head. I cried. I waited. Nothing. I explained to him what had happened and when he spoke, his voice was bitter.

It's as if what happened to me made him lose his love for me.

"You are educated," Dr. Patag told my mister, "You can't blame your wife because she saved you from dying. It's not that she wanted to be used like that. You should be ashamed."

My mister nodded his head. And then he wept. He held our son out to me so I could hold him. He told the doctor he would take me home and that he didn't have to worry about me because in our town there were seven doctors. He wanted to know what he owed the doctor, but the doctor told him to never mind. "I did this for Mrs. Lorenzo. Anyway, the government pays me."

My mister took me home, but he did not forgive me.

"I said to God," she tells me, pulling a thread out of her blouse, "if he no longer loves me, maybe it's better I die."

After a long moment, she grabs my hands and then tosses them aside. I jump at the sudden movement. She turns away from me and looks into the camera. "Peace time, peace time," she is muttering. "What do you think? Do you think we have forgotten what has happened? Every day we wake up and it's in our head. Every night we go to sleep, and it is with us again. What do you think, when we sleep, do you think we forget? It is always with us, these memories, this destruction. Even now, it is here." She points to her head, staring at the camera lens like she is going to shoot herself. Her arm begins swinging back and forth. Her long and bony finger shakes at the camera lens. "Where is our justice? Where is our apology? How long must we wait?" she wants to know. "Panay hearings, always hearings. More hearings. Tell us once and for all, what will you do? Yes or no? So we know what to do!"

I know she's talking about the Japanese government. I know she means that the women of LILA Pilipina have filed countless suits against the Japanese government. But the Japanese government is not the only culprit. Remember? The Filipinos were quiet until the Americans came and made a playground out of their country. And who are the Americans? Does she mean the soldiers who fought in World War II? Does she mean the U.S. soldiers returning in 2001 in the name of terrorism? Does she mean the Dalaga Project—the five young women from America and me?

From the moment the dalagas and I arrive, she challenges us. She wants to know how true our intentions are. She plants a seed in me that will take root and grow amid my own tangled branches as I define to myself who I am—the oldest daughter of Filipino immigrants, a single woman making her own path, a teacher, a writer, a sister, an American-born Filipina—a very tall and crooked-curvy tree with branches turning in every direction. In the years to come I visit the lolas often. I hear the stories told to me once, twice, three times. I go on marches and then return to my life in Miami. It may seem as though I am forgetting. But I cannot. And I am not. Even as I teach my workshops and direct the program here at the university, the politics rise up and often I take to the web and other public venues. Every time the Japanese government refuses the lolas I respond. After all, Lola Catalina Lorenzo is my kababayan. Her father and my father are both from Macabebe. More than anything, I want her to see me as I am and to trust me.

Dalaga project on the Go

June 16–August 11, 1999

Mondays	Integration Days	Antipolo, Navotas, Metro Manila
Tuesdays	Language Days	Lolas' House, Quezon City
Wednesdays	Drama/Dance Days	Lolas' House, Quezon City
Thursdays	Art/Music Days	Lolas' House, Quezon City

WE STAY AT St. Scholastica's College in Malate. Every morning we drive through thick traffic to get to Quezon City and Lolas' House, where we spend our afternoons with the women of LILA Pilipina. We want to build friendships with the lolas. On language days we sit on the patio and draw images from the market, or the sea, or the classroom, and we label them in English and Tagalog. In this way we teach each other to speak. On drama days we do short improvisations with the lolas, acting out skits that demonstrate to us and to them in what ways we were alike and in what ways our American attitudes made us different. On art days we throw a canvas on a table and pull out all kinds of paints and brushes. We sit next to one another and paint whatever we want. Most lolas paint nipa huts—their houses in the country—or Japanese soldiers—their captors. On dance days, the lolas and dalagas teach each other their favorite dances—everything from the tango and the cha-cha to hip-hop and how to raise the roof. All these activities take place on the Lolas' House patio. And on integration days, we venture to their communities and each of the six of us spends a day with a lola in her home. In this way, we become friends. We not only hear their stories of the past, but we enjoy their playful spirits in song, dance, and art. In this way, we become their apo.

And one day, they ask us point-blank, "When are you going to interview us?" And so we do.

Dalaga project

Lolas' House, Quezon City, Metro Manila
July 1999

FIRST COMES THE knock at the door. Timid. Small, like a tree branch scratching the side of the house. The door creaks open and a little gray head pushes into the room. The voice, soft as the knocking, "Ako na?" My turn?

Ana Fe zooms the lens out as I usher the small woman into the room. Lola sniffs at my face and kisses me. She seizes Ana Fe and wraps herself around Ana Fe's body. The two laugh, look into each other's eyes, and squint. They mirror one another for a moment, a little dance. Ana Fe lets out a hearty laugh. I gesture to a plastic chair facing the camera. "Sige, Lola," I tell her. Ana Fe seats Lola in the chair and slips a lavalier microphone onto the lapel of her dress, a floral patterned print, bright and cheery.

I place myself across from her, next to the camcorder locked down on the tripod. Ana Fe scoots her way behind me and fits headphones squarely onto her skull. She frames Lola in the shot.

Lola looks right into the camera, states her name, age, and where she was born. Then, halfway through the testimony, her eye wanders and glances at me.

She places a hand on my knee as she describes the day she was abducted. She draws the scene—a rice field, a schoolyard, the middle of a church. She peoples the story with her family, her schoolmates, her neighbors. She places herself in the scenario and as the soldiers come out of nowhere, her voice quickens, and tears follow. Lola slips away from English and into Tagalog. And as the story turns to rape, her Tagalog shifts into the dialect of her village. To the Japanese soldiers she

27

assigns a made-up dialog. "Kura! Kura!" they said. "Kura! Kura!" When Lola tells the story she relives the trauma and the languages blur. Ana Fe and I begin to cry. Then, Lola grabs my hand and brings me to the scars and I witness her history there, on her body, with my fingers and I say, "Yes, Lola, it's still crooked." Lola and I collapse into a long embrace. Ana Fe leaves her post behind the camera, and, reaching her arms around us, holds us as the three of us weep into each other's arms.

Then come the heavy sighs. The stuttered breathing. The wiping of eyes. The leaning one into the other as if to help each other stand. Then comes the calming. The murmurs. The hiccups. And when Lola is calm, when the hem of her skirt has been soaked by not only her tears but also Ana Fe's and mine, we give her a kiss on the cheek. We take a breath with her. We ask for her blessing and whisper, "Okay na?" And when she nods, we open the door and set her free.

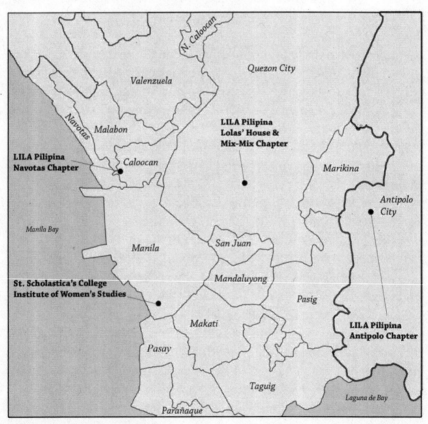

Dalaga Project Locations

Then, Ana Fe and I exchange a look. There is the faintest tapping on the door. And soon the next lola enters, then the next. We continue until fifteen women have been interviewed.

Eight hours later, Tara, Neleh, Lizzie, and Eliza arrive. On the dark patio the lolas have already begun dancing. The girls take one look at me and Ana Fe. My head throbs from all the crying. My eyes are red and swollen.

"You guys," Tara says. "What's wrong?"

Every joint and every limb of our bodies is sore. We don't answer. The four dalagas come to us then, circling us, embracing us, breathing with us.

Lola Regina pokes her head out of the kitchen, takes one look at us, and says, "The stories have entered their bodies."

VIRGINIA VILLARMA
Bureau of Customs, Office of the Commissioner
June 7, 2002

Born May 5, 1929

Abducted by the Imperial
Japanese Army, 1943,
Intramuros, Metro Manila

Testimony of Virginia Villarma

I am Lola Virgie. I was born on May 5, 1929. I was orphaned when I was two years old and brought to Manila before the war. I was a vendor for my uncle near the river in Delpan.

Fourteen years old, I was not thinking of war because we were so poor. When the Japanese first came, we lived in Intramuros. They captured the civilians and my uncle was not spared.

For a long time there was no food and people were dying of hunger. So one day, for my aunt, I went across the street, searching for food. Five Japanese soldiers on a jeep stopped. I ran but because they were looking for women, they came after me. When they caught me, I struggled. They held my hands down and I thought that they would kill me. They pulled my hair. They jabbed my back with their bayonets. They hauled me onto the jeep like a pig bound for market. They kicked me. They pulled me up only to throw me down again. They drove me to what is now the customs house. We took a turn near Jones Bridge and headed south to the garrison. I thought they would kill me.

When we got there, they put me in a room with many other prisoners. I didn't recognize any of the women. I wanted to get out, but there was nothing I could do, so I cried. The Japanese soldiers undressed me. And because they were still pointing their guns at me, I was scared. I could do nothing but resign myself to what they were doing.

I suffered for months, and sometimes when I think of it I can still feel the pain. When I was there, they would not feed me. I'd wait for leftovers from those who pitied me. The soldiers made me wash their clothes and clean their sleeping quarters.

I suffered for three months. Until one day there was a riot. The Japanese could not determine who was their enemy. Everyone ran. I crawled under the barbed-wire fence. And then I ran toward the Pasig River. I had no idea if I was being followed, but I ran as if I were. When I got to the river, I jumped in. I hid under a water lily floating among the grass and I rested. And slowly, I began to move underwater. But I did not know how to swim and I was afraid they'd see me in the water. So I crawled through the water slowly. I don't know how, but I floated to the other side of the river, which was big and wide. By then I was not afraid anymore. I didn't care if I drowned. I was more afraid that they might catch me again.

When I reached the other side, I saw people and I was scared because I thought they were Japanese, but they were civilians. And when I rose from the water, I was surprised to see my dress was torn from the barbed-wire fence and my skin too. Blood flowed from my wound. I was bleeding everywhere. I felt nothing. The people bandaged me up.

By the time I was well enough to look for my aunt she had evacuated from Manila, so two couples adopted me. I worked for them, sewing clothes. Later, when I found my aunt, I didn't tell her what had happened to me because I was ashamed.

Hilot Lolas

WHEN WE ARRIVE at Lolas' House, our backpacks full of bottled water, blank tapes, and cameras charged and ready to go, the women greet us, blessing each dalaga with a kiss, an embrace, and a battery of sweet and indiscernible words. It's a little like Christmas.

Lola Regina has her hands on Lizzie, who looks particularly sleepy. She looks up into the girl's face, examines the silver stud on her lip. She puts her finger on it and says, "Hindi masakit?"

"She wants to know if your stud hurts," I say.

"Naw, you get used to it," Lizzie answers. "Good morning, Lola."

Lola Regina runs her hands over the array of little clips. Lizzie has rolled her pixie haircut into a million pin curls. She looks into her face. The girl's lids droop and her dark eyes hide behind the slits. Her skin has broken out into a little sweat. The old woman brushes the hair back with her hands, though every short hair has already been pinned back by the clips. "May sakit siya?" Lola Regina asks me.

"Siguro pagod lang," I say. "She doesn't sleep enough. Are you feeling okay?"

Lizzie shrugs and her skinny shoulders rise up to her ears, "My head aches."

"Masakit ang ulo niya," I inform Lola Regina, who has already pulled a plastic chair up and is guiding Lizzie to sit. From her pocket, Lola Regina takes out a tiny jar of tiger balm and covers her palms with it. She rubs her hands together and blows.

"Did you eat breakfast this morning?" I ask her. "Maybe it's a hunger headache."

The girls gather around Lola Regina and Lizzie. Lola wraps her hands around Lizzie's broad forehead, closing her own eyes and muttering to herself. She rubs the cool balm on Lizzie's temples. The scent of mint leaves and other healing herbs waft from the circle. Lizzie's shoulders relax. The muscles on her face go soft.

"Oh that feels good," Lizzie says, her vowels flat and nasal. "What are you doing?"

Throughout our stay, the lolas know when we're not well, when our stomachs are weak, or our heads are bursting with pain, and they pull us aside. And it seems it is always a different lola—sometimes Prescila, sometimes Josefa or Regina—always a different lola. They take their hands, hands that have laundered other's dirty clothes, hands that have cooked in dirty kitchens of the richest homes, hands that have delivered dozens of babies, hands that have wrapped fresh fish in newspaper and sold them in the markets, hands that have suffered the touch of unwanted men, and they heal us. We don't question them. We don't push them away. We sit on the chair or we lie on the cot and we open up our hearts, just like that, trusting them and their magic ways, their lovely hands—old hands, rough hands, healing hands.

LUCIA ALVAREZ

Born February 12, 1925,
Samar Island, Visayas

Abducted by the Imperial
Japanese Army, October 1944,
Samar Island, Visayas

Testimony of Lucia Alvarez

Lolas' House, Quezon City
July 1999

Thank you. I owe Ritchie. She paid for my haircut. Should I start? Are you ready? I am Lucia Alvarez. Do you want to know where I was born? I was born on the island of Samar—and my birthdate?—February 12, 1925. So my story, like this—In 1941, when I was sixteen years old I fell in love and I married into a family who loved me. By the following year I had given birth to a baby girl. Because they thought I was beautiful and because they loved me, my in-laws pampered me. We lived with them so I could stay home with the baby.

After the war began, our family moved to an evacuation center in the mountains. In October of 1944, I heard my mother-in-law screaming one day. I ran to her and saw my husband being beaten by Japanese soldiers. They punched him. They boxed his ears; they poked his chest with the bayonet swords. Blood ran down his chest and covered his clothing. I could see how badly they wanted to kill him.

"Let's go to the mayor," my mother-in-law said. "Let's get him to help. He's the mayor, isn't he?"

So I snuck out the door, and before I could run, the Japanese who were beating my husband saw me. They dropped my husband and left him for dead and began to carry me away.

I resisted, even though they pulled me with both arms. They had to drag my body because I would not go. Tapos, I lost my

37

balance. I fell and hit a large stone and broke the joint here [*she stretches out her left arm and points to the inside of her elbow*]. I cried out and instead of helping me up, they pushed me. They were irritated that I fell. They pulled me. When they saw that my arm was broken, they tied my limb up in a sling. They shouted to me in words that I could not understand. I wiped the tears from my eyes with my right hand and saw blood.

I cried and I cried the entire walk. I could not stop. I cried even as I climbed the hill to the seminary doors of St. Vincent DePaul in Calbayog. The soldiers threw me in a room. They stripped me of my clothes and left me naked for a week. Yes, naked. So it was easier for them when they raped me. Each time soldiers felt the urge, they simply barged into the room—two soldiers at a time—and holding a gun nearby, they used me. My body was so dirty. My arm so swollen with infection. I could not bear the severe pain. I would scream every time they came near me because the pain was so great. And also, I lost the movement in my right hand, it was so swollen.

"Look," the Japanese soldiers told me, "If you don't like what we're doing, we'll kill you."

After one week, they gave me back my clothing. But for a month, I suffered the same abuse. My infected arm was left in that sling. The pain was so unbearable, I only remember the constant stream of tears falling. They raped me constantly. I couldn't bear the pain of this. [*She indicates the broken arm, the bruised palm of her right hand.*]

Two Japanese soldiers and three Filipino soldiers, Visayans, stood watch over me. And every time the Japanese entered the room, the Filipinos left me there, all alone.

After a month, I noticed a silence. Where were the soldiers? The only ones who entered the room were the Visayan soldiers. The raping had finally ended. And soon, not even the Visayan soldiers were coming into the room.

I snuck out the door, I peeked around the corner, looking. Nothing. No people. I found my way to the seashore and looked for soldiers. No one. I looked across the water and saw my parents' barrio.

My parents welcomed me home and treated my arms and my hands. They gave me medicine, and they brought healers to fix my bones and my disjointed elbow. In some ways, it was too late. The pain had become a permanent part of my body. If you don't take care of these things right away, they stay with you forever.

When my husband heard I was alive, he came to me. A month had already gone by. I saw a weak man, sickly with wounds of the war. But I loved him and I went with him.

You know, my in-laws thought I was dead. So when they saw me, they were so happy. Because my husband was weak, he could not work. And so our parents took us both in. You know they loved me very much—I was younger then—and I was rounder and prettier. I had a look.

Drawing Day

WE TOSS A blank tarp over the long tables and scatter plastic cups of water and Styrofoam palettes of blues and greens and reds across the canvas. We throw down brushes like a dare and we invite the lolas to join us. The dalagas take them by the hand and seat them to their left and right and across from them. The language barriers have cracked and we are creating new words as we smile and laugh, as we use our whole bodies to gesture a little joke.

I unfold the viewfinder on my camcorder and power up, strolling down the long table and peeking over everyone's shoulder. The sun enters the patio at an angle and so the light surrounds them like a golden halo and the colors rise like ribbons of smoke. Today we work in silence, lost in the colors and the shapes. Lola Lucia hunches over her space on the table, the brush pointed like a pen. She leans close to the table, painting a figure that is equally as round as she is. She breathes with each stroke and the colors wash one into the other—a soft blue and yellow, a startling red. There are no details and yet somehow, the figure mirrors her body and the colors swim into each other, happy and free. I shoot over her shoulder so that the lens can see her gray head and the glitter of a silver hair band and the brushstrokes on the canvas. All her concentration is there on that body.

"Sino ba yan?" I ask her, pointing to the figure.

"Si Lucy," she tells me.

"Sino?"

"Si Lucy, ako."

"Ikaw?" I say, practically singing to her. "You are so beautiful. She looks just like you."

She laughs when I say this. Her whole body expands just a little.

The lolas and dalagas paint their self-portraits in nonlinear spaces, their figures overlapping with one another and their lives growing out of the figures. There are nipa huts and rivers and palm trees. There are soldiers and bayonets and jeeps of women being taken away. There are flowers and fish and words: Mahal. Lola. Dalaga. Laban!

When I pick up the pen to draw myself, I choose a thin black marker and I make a stick figure with long arms and legs. I stretch the length of the canvas from one end of the table to the other and I hold in my stick-figure arms each of the little lolas who come to my shoulder, some to my jaw, some hit the spot at the space of my heart, and in-between the lolas, you can see the stick-figure shapes of girls just becoming women. I draw little flames in the center of their chests. I draw their faces in—not circles or ovals like faces should be, but hearts with fat cheeks and pointy chins and hair parted down the middle. I am gathering them up like pencils and I am holding them tight and I am aching from the center of my chest. The black dots that I have drawn on my face for eyes blur as the ink runs. I try to blot the eyes dry.

Every day there is a new drama going on with the girls or with the lolas or with the organizers. Some misunderstanding. Some offense. Eliza has shut down and her face goes cold every time she sees me. She spends her time with her head bowed, scribbling furiously onto pads of paper. She writes her mother, missing her in ways she never knew were possible. She thought she was going home, but she has discovered that everything has changed. This is not home. What we're doing here is not what she expected. The lolas do not touch her in the same ways they move the other girls, or maybe they do move her in such deep ways she cannot express.

I try talking with her, but she refuses to look at me. Her eyes are set on an object far from here and my words circle her, but they do not enter her. "Do you want to stay?" I ask her. "Do you want to go?" No answer. No answer.

She is the little one in the drawing, the one I dress in baggy pants and a tight T-shirt and a big satchel. She is the one with a vacant expression on her heart-shaped face.

Normally, I would have made myself the tall writer, dancing, my legs kicking at the air, my arms floating like kite strings. I would have been alone and happy. I would have had a notebook in my hand and one of those gel pens. I would have been free to go anywhere. But today, I draw myself with these long arms and feet that are rooted to the earth and toes that are digging into the dirt, and I am gathering people next to me, holding them up and holding them together and I can feel my heart cracking, but I brace myself and I say, no, no, no, not now.

Estela Adriatico
March 1, 2002

Laban! Laban! Laban!

On the Move to Commonwealth Avenue
July 26, 1999

FOR YEARS, THE lolas have been attending the president's State of the Nation Address—not as guests, but as protestors. Today, the organizers advise me and the dalagas to bring only what we can carry. To wear closed-toed shoes. Bring water, the organizers tell us. Be ready to run.

At Lolas' House thirty old women have gathered. They wear the purple T-shirts of LILA Pilipina. Scarves and straw hats protect their fragile scalps from the hot sun. The staff members pass around little bundles of food—our baon should we get hungry—two pickled eggs, saging, rice, a bottle of water.

Our van drives down Commonwealth Avenue in Quezon City. My eyes search the streets. We caravan with two other jeepneys of lolas. I watch as they hang the LILA Pilipina banner out the side of the truck's open doorway. The flag unfurls in the sun, wipes the sky clean of Manila smog. From the front seat, I see the lolas' fists raised. They are excited, too.

Someone stops the jeepneys ahead of us. The police will not allow the drivers to continue. Only private cars are allowed to go farther. Since we have hired a van on our own, we take part in the protest by shuttling the lolas back and forth from the point of entry to the entrance where we expect to see President Estrada driving past.

What a sight. Up on the curve the police stand, their bulletproof shields held out in front of them, their sunglasses blocking out the bright sun, their helmets keeping their heads safe from bottles, or bricks, or the fists of angry lolas. Below them, lolas line up. They set their stools down. They pull out their signs and umbrellas. Some of them crack salted eggs open or peel bananas.

Ana Fe shoots everything she sees, camcorder to eye, a big grin across her face. Neleh grabs the LILA banner from one of the organizers and holds it up, resists the pull of the wind. The pole is as tall as she is and the banner the size of a twin bed. She stands with her legs firmly rooted to the street and her chest pushing out at the crowd, and she says to the girls, "Evelina should be the one holding this. She's the tallest one."

I take the banner. For the most part I am silent, absorbing the spectacle, memorizing the colors around me. Adrenaline courses through my body and I find myself swaying to the chant of the protesters. I am drawn to the revolution, but I don't know what to do. My body feels so tall and out of place, my arms and legs awkward. My accent so American.

The protest program begins, and all the organizations—of workers and farmers and poor people—take turns at the bullhorn. They shout their grievances to the crowd, they call out to the absent president. Young radical poets and musicians sing songs of revolution into the coveted bullhorn, accompanied by acoustic guitars. They wait for Estrada to hear their pleas. Meanwhile, the lolas hold umbrellas over their heads to keep them from baking in the sun.

Lola Lucia glances at me from underneath the wide brim of her hat. I see a tear in her eye and I wrap my arms around her and I hold her. She rests her head on my chest. The wind blows and she mouths something to me, but the noise around us is so loud. I pop open her raggedy umbrella to shade us both from the scorching sun. "What is that?" I ask her. "Anong klaseng umbrella ba ito?" There is a cigarette burn in the middle of the umbrella and the sun sizzles right through it. Lola laughs.

Other lolas begin to sit down right on the curb at the feet of the police. Young officers lean over and tell them little jokes, flirting with them like naughty sons. One policeman calls, "Take my picture, Evelyn!" Like every other Filipino I have met this summer, he has changed my name from Evelina to Evelyn. How does he know who I am? Most likely one of the lolas told him. He waves at me, smiling. At lunchtime, the policemen's food arrives in Styrofoam takeout plates. Rice and chicken. They discard their shields, helmets, and sunglasses like children breaking character from a game of make-believe. Their toys

44

litter the ground. They sit down any place they can, their legs spread wide apart, their boyish faces smiling as they eat their lunches.

Then a hand from the flatbed reaches down into the crowd and pulls Lola Narcisa up onto the truck. Unlike the other lolas in their T-shirts, she has on a pair of black trousers and a gray-and-black plaid top. She takes the bullhorn, holds it up to her mouth with one hand, and with the other she gestures to the sky. Her body rocks back and forth as she speaks and as she does the crowd roars. She knows when to speak and when to pause, she knows how to listen to the revolution. "LABAN!" shout the lolas from the curb. "LABAN! LABAN! LABAN!" FIGHT! FIGHT! FIGHT!

LABAN MGA LOLA! In that moment, I do not hesitate. My body buzzes from all the energy around me. The words wash over me and the sun heats my skin so my body browns like the color of coconut husk. Lola Lucia and I hold our fists up to the sky and she rears her head back, the hat nearly falling, mouth open and laughter spilling out. The cry of the "comfort women."

July 2, 2002

State of the Nation Address protest, July 26, 1999

Virginia Villarma
July 12, 2002

Prescila Bartonico
March 1, 2002

Her Name Means Light

WHEN I HEARD of the death of Lola Lucia Alvarez, I searched my notebooks, my bins of paperwork. I spun a monsoon in my little office. I was in search of her self-portrait, a marker drawing scratched onto a purple note card. Stuck in the middle of America, I felt so far away from her and all the lolas. I found her in the pages of the summer's travel journal. She had rendered herself a messy stick figure with a cocked left foot. She had made herself a little skirt. Maybe she was dancing. For when Lola Lucia warmed up to us, she danced.

Once I caught Lola Lucia and our two hip-hop-clad dalagas running up the hill on Matimpiin Street. Lizzie and Eliza held onto one of Lola Lucia's fat little arms, while an umbrella magically hovered above them. It was rainy season and everything around them was gray except the trees and the grass, which were a brilliant green. Smoke trailed up into the sky as each of them puffed on the same cigarette, handing the stick from one hand to the next. And when I called out to them, all three glanced back at me and started trotting up the hill, laughing.

Next to her stick figure she had penned her name in blue ink: LUCIA ALVAREZ. On the bottom of the card were two purple ink marks. Each of the marks had four legs. Next to one she had written "pusa." Next to the other, she had scrawled "aso." The pictures of the cat and dog are identical.

Lola Lucia, unlike the other lolas, lived in Lolas' House on Matimpiin Street because she had no other place. She was the seventy-four-year-old errand girl for LILA Pilipina. Lola Regina was also living there at the time, but that was because her home was far away in the provinces. Every week, for eight weeks, while Lola Regina read our palms or healed our headaches with her Tiger Balm and magic, Lola Lucia was sent to pick up cold bottles of orange Royal, Coca-Cola, and hot biscuits of pan de sal. She was given the task to run to the copy center or deposit money into the bank. She was the one they asked to buy envelopes. When it was rainy season and there was baha, Lola Lucia was the one who took a pail to the floor and scooped water out bucket by bucket. Other lolas came to Lolas' House seeking temporary refuge from their families or housemates. They came when they were lonely, or when the memories of war were too much to bear. Sometimes they came looking for LILA Pilipina staff to help them decipher legal or medical paperwork. They came one or several at a time. But Lola Lucia lived and worked there.

ON SUNDAY, NOVEMBER 28, 1999, sixty lolas boarded jeepneys to protest the actions of the Third Informal ASEAN Summit. When I hear of events that occurred at that rally, I recall the protests we had been to that summer. How the Philippine National Police (PNP) acted more like grandsons to the women than military police. I think of the lolas and the way they persevered the heat and the exhaustion, just to make their fight known. I cannot imagine why the police would threaten to harm the lolas.

Once the lolas arrived at the Philippine International Convention Center, they were met by a blockade of police who would not allow them to protest. Volunteers of LILA Pilipina were able to negotiate five minutes for the lolas, and as they disembarked from the jeepneys and pulled out their placards and bullhorn, PNP officer Cabigon ordered them to evacuate. The police lined up, holding out their shields. They demanded the lolas retreat by the count of five or they would be forced to, in their words "hurt" the lolas. "Masaktan kayo!" they yelled. Some of the police were armed with guns. The lolas began moving, but they weren't moving fast enough for the police. "Tulak! Tulak!" the police yelled to one another. Ritchie told the police to be patient with the lolas. "They're old," she told them, "They cannot move quickly." Still they pushed and pushed. During this time, Lola Lucia was heard saying, "Ninerbyos ako dahil sa pulis." *The police are making me nervous.*

After the lolas boarded the jeepneys, the drivers were ordered to stay on Roxas Boulevard. The jeepneys began to take the sixty lolas away but were caught in heavy traffic. During this time more police stopped the caravan, claiming the drivers were not licensed to be in the area. They confiscated the drivers' licenses and threatened to arrest them. The lolas told the police they would not take the drivers alone; they would have to arrest them, too.

The jeepneys were led to a local police station in Pasay City where the lolas took advantage of a vacant lot nearby and began their program of protest. During this time, Lola Lucia felt severe pains in her neck and head. When staff members requested the police release one of the drivers to take Lola Lucia to the hospital, they refused, saying it was not their commander's orders. She would have to wait.

The PNP detained Lola Lucia fifteen minutes after her attack began.

Finally, a LILA staff member was able to secure a taxi and took Lola Lucia to San Juan de Dios Hospital in Pasay City. Even as she was being taken into the ICU, Lola Lucia was saying, "Gusto kong lumaban!" *I want to fight.* Shortly after her arrival at the hospital, Lola Lucia slipped into a five-day coma and died.

There was no money for her burial or for the expense of her hospital stay.

I HEAR THIS news from the other side of the ocean and anger sends me flipping through my photos, holding tight to every image I have of Lola Lucia. Her self-portrait sits next to me even now. Of course it looks nothing like her. It's an ink drawing, a stick figure. I imagine her running up and down the streets of Quezon City, an envelope under one arm, a kerchief wiping her brow.

Her name means light. Those Japanese soldiers thought they had hauled in a virgin—something sweet, inexperienced, fresh. But she was a wife and a mother. Lucia Alvarez was a grown woman who knew better than to test her captors while they stripped her and raped her over and over again. She knew she had a choice, to stay quiet and live or to resist and feel the bullet. She chose to be quiet. She chose to settle things afterward and in her own way.

Had she known it would be her last protest, would Lola Lucia have boarded the jeepney anyway? Of course she would have. She'd have gone just for the chance to make her case known. She probably wouldn't have said anything to the Japanese prime minister, but she would have stood there. Maybe she'd stretch her limp arm out so he could see the damaged joint, turn her body in circles to reveal her swollen backside. She would have looked him in the eye, so he could see the sadness for all the things her life could never be. She would have gazed at him silently, her soft light revealing everything.

Closer to Home

THE FIRST TIME I went to the Philippines, I was under two years old. I have a sepia-toned photo—a wide shot of my parents walking across the tarmac at Manila International Airport. We are walking away from the nose of our airplane, its fat wings sweeping out of the frame, and behind us is the long staircase we have just descended. My mother leads us in her stylish Jackie O way; my father follows closely behind. He is wearing a dark suit, white shirt, and tie. You can see his black, plastic-rimmed glasses. You can see his wide smile and the deep dimples that are a signature Galang trait. You can see me, a toddler in a dress and pixie haircut, nesting in the crook of his arm. We are coming home, walking toward the building where more than a hundred members of our clan are gathered on the balconies, waving at us. You can see their shadows on the ground. We are coming home, though I have never been here before.

The second time I went was with the Dalaga Project, thirty-seven years later. I have no memories of being in the Philippines before this trip—only vague images that pass before me when I'm not thinking. Santol on my tongue is a sweet and sour memory. Humidity on my skin is like the breath of my love—familiar, warm, intimate, mine. And the clamor of one hundred voices, the laughter and the chime of their two hundred pieces of silverware on china, are home. This is home. But I am working and I arrive with five young women who are my charges, and I cannot let my guard down. I have forty old women marching in the street before me, I have no time for myself, save the short weekends when I return to Bituan or Macopa or the house in Macabebe.

What become mine are the visits. Each night, when I am lying in my bed in Malate and close my eyes, a thousand faces visit me. They bloom in the dark like smoke billowing in the sky. The faces are sometimes fine line drawings of light, but mostly they pass before me like clouds. One after the other. Old men with crooked noses. Mothers with full faces and masses of hair. Grandmothers looking wrinkled like old trees. Little baby faces, eyes closed, mouths open. Faces, only faces. They come to me each night. Remind me I am home. I know them though I've never met them.

The third time I go to the Philippines, in 2001, the Twin Towers in New York City have just crumbled to the ground and the world has changed. No one knows what will become of us after 9/11. I am not sure that I want to go, but I have been given a Fulbright Senior Research Scholar award and it is an opportunity to visit the lolas and redeem my promise. I can tell their stories. I can help them fight for justice. After waking up alone one morning in Iowa and witnessing the plumes of smoke rising on television, I leave my family in Milwaukee. Three of my siblings here have just had babies—two girls and a boy—and I must go without seeing the first year of their lives. I go. This time, I am without my parents, without the dalagas. I go.

PILAR FRIAS

Born October 5, 1926,
Anib, Sipucot, Camarines Sur, Bicol

Abducted by the Imperial
Japanese Army, 1943, Bikol

Filed Postwar Compensation Suit,
September 1993,
Tokyo District Court

Testimony of Pilar Frias

The Life of a "Comfort Woman"

The life of a "comfort woman" is hard
I have suffered all hardships
Oh the path that I have walked!
To sleep on cement floors, not even a mat beneath me.

To suffer quietly this life
At the hands of Japanese soldiers
The life of the "comfort woman" is hard
And the cause of my suffering is war

And that is why we should demand
To stop all wars
War destroys our womanhood
Some are raped and others killed

And that is why we should proclaim
An end to all wars
Because the life of "comfort women" is hard
And the cause of all our suffering is war

I am Lola Pilar Frias. I was born on October 5, 1926, in Anib, Sipucot, Camarines Sur, Bicol. I'm seventy-three years old now.

When the Japanese arrived in 1942, my father was the baranggay captain of our village. We had two houses—one in the barrio and the other on a farm. We had a big coconut farm. Now, when my father and mother went to the barrio, they left me with my mother's youngest sister. My aunt was twenty years old. I was sixteen. We were the only ones left on the coconut farm.

At ten in the evening, we heard gunshots. That's how the Japanese announced their arrival—they'd fire their guns at the sky—and that's how we knew they were in the barrio. Then they'd go from house to house. They'd take the pigs, kill them, and eat them. They took my father's chickens in the backyard. Anyway, when I heard the gunshots I went to my aunt, who was washing clothes in a giant drum of water. Each day we'd fill it by noon because that was when they'd shut the water down. I told her about the gunfire.

By and by, five Japanese soldiers came. Our farmhouse was not so far from the barrio. Maybe fifty meters. When the Japanese got to our farm, my aunt was sweeping the yard and it was my turn to wash the clothes. Two of the Japanese came to me and said, "Kura! Kura!" The others went to my aunt but I don't know what they told her. They told me, "Kura! Kura!" Civilian spy. I was wondering what "kura kura" meant. I felt so afraid. It was the first time I had ever seen the Japanese. I was afraid. I was told kura kura and I didn't know how to answer. So do you know what one did? He burned my face with a cigarette butt. I shouted because it hurt. When I shouted, he took a hunting knife with its sharp point and he attacked me here. You see this? This one here. [*She indicates a scar along the side of her nose.*]

Yes, Lola.

And also here. Feel it. Go like this. The scar goes through here. You see?

Yes, Lola. I see it.

You feel it? Here. The skin was hanging like this, suspended on my face. There was blood. I cried because I didn't know what else to do. Then the soldier pulled my hair and pushed me into that drum of water. You know, the one we used for washing clothes. The Japanese soldier got angry because I shouted and then he attacked me with his knife. Blood was everywhere, then he shoved my head back in the water again. That cut was that big. Just hanging there like it was going to fall off. He almost hit my neck, but I moved and so he hit my face instead.

I used eggplant leaves as medicine. I pressed them into the open wounds but it never really healed. I couldn't go to the doctors back then because it was the Japanese occupation. It took more than two months to heal. Twenty years later and it was still painful. Unbearable. I couldn't touch it. Not even after twenty years.

After the five Japanese soldiers captured me and my aunt, they tied us to a jackfruit tree. The tree is still standing in our backyard, even today. There, they raped us. In the barrio, a clarinet sounded and when the soldiers heard it, they took my father's roosters and brought them to the barrio.

The Japanese soldiers went to the mountain to look for Filipino guerrilla camps. Our barrio had many guerrillas and they would come during the week—Monday through Saturday. So the Japanese were always coming into our village, looking for them.

After a month, the Japanese told us to leave the barrio, so we moved to Cabusao in 1943, I think. When we went back in 1944, all of our houses had been burned down. Even the church.

Two families were living in the school—one was an old couple. We had heard if you lived on the coconut farm, that's where you were supposed to go. But when we got there, the Japanese were in the school. We tried to hide, but we didn't know where to go because there was only one building and the soldiers were all around. That was how they caught us—when we were trying to hide.

The Japanese soldiers held three men and three women. The men were cooking for the soldiers and serving them lunch. There was a big tent and the men had cooking utensils, rice, and canned goods. The women, however, were tied around their waists so they would not escape.

After lunch, Captain Takagi—that was his name, Takagi; he was tall—after lunch he ordered his men to go. He made the civilians leave, too. He ordered his men to tie me and bring me with them and they tied me up along with the three women.

We walked toward the mountain. It was a long walk. We arrived in the evening and stopped near the river. Maybe it was five o'clock. The forest was thick with big trees and large trunks. It was so dark. The soldiers were looking for guerrillas. They were in search of the camp, but I knew we had already passed it. We walked such a distance and when we finally stopped, they cooked porridge and sardines in a big pan. After the soldiers finished eating, they gave us leftovers. Then they made us lie down on the ground and that is where we slept. That night we were raped again. Five Japanese raped each of us.

Five?

Yes, the other Japanese soldiers were roaming around, as if guarding. They had light and it shone like a spot.

Like a flashlight?

Yes, a flashlight.

The next day, we walked along the river. But before we left, we washed Japanese soldiers' clothes and shoes. Then they found the guerrilla camp, but no one was there. It looked like they recently left because we found newly cut coconut on the grounds. The Japanese kept us at that camp, then, for a month. They turned it into their garrison and that is where they raped us every night. When a group of Japanese soldiers left the camp, another group would come—maybe fifty soldiers—and when they left another would come, and so on and so on.

We could not escape until one night we heard planes flying overhead. That was when the Japanese soldiers left the camp— when there were rumors they had surrendered. We had to follow them to the barrio because we didn't know our way. The forest was so thick. And even as we followed the soldiers, we girls remained tied at the waist. One of the civilian men tried to untie us but could not, so he burned the knot. We followed the

Japanese from a distance because we feared they might take us again. We were maybe fifty meters behind them when we heard trucks. It was 1944 and the Japanese were heading to Legaspi. There were so many. When we got to the highway we stopped following them.

That was how I got out of the guerrilla camp. My mother thought I was dead. That is all my story. That is my statement.

The Life of a "Comfort Woman"

LOLA PILAR FRIAS welcomes most guests by singing "Buhay ng 'Comfort Woman,'" a lament she composed about her life as a survivor. The minor melody haunts me. It is the summer of 2008, and tonight one of my charges from Florida has brought other Filipino America students to the new Lolas' Center on Narra Street to meet the lolas. Lola Pilar croons her song with one hand hanging by her side and the other moving to the rhythm of the music. She sways gently, stepping left and right in an easy dance. Her head tilts as if leaning on someone for support. From where I sit, I can't tell there's a scar slicing down the side of her nose. Her smile stretches across her face, despite the sad song, her eyes light up as she looks at each person in the audience. Her shoulders hunch over ever so slightly. Her waistline rides high, nearly to her bust.

When I was a child, my father cut out a string of paper dolls for me. I held the first one by the hand and waved her in the air. Identical in shape and color, the other dolls floated after her, forever attached. I think of those dolls every time I hear Lola Pilar's testimony. I think of what that might have been like to be strung together from the waist in the middle of a war. Every time you fell, the others would fall. Every time you had to defecate, the others would be right next to you. Every time you were raped, the other three were there, waiting their turn. Now, Lola's waist cinches up as if it still holds the memory of that rope jerking her body left and right. Her bloody wounds have healed and her beautiful nose sprawls flat and unevenly across her face.

After Lola Pilar's song, each lola and each visitor stands up and introduces herself or himself. Every now and then, one of the Fil-Am students also breaks into song. The lolas clap. And then we eat the meal I have prepared—chicken adobo, rice, and pansit. It is the first time since I met them nine years ago that I have cooked for them. The students have brought the lolas bottles of wine. Afterward, the music plays and all the lolas choose one of the students and together they dance for hours. Lola Pilar, who has had a glass or two of wine, spins round in circles. She grabs hold of other lolas, twirls them. A Filipino American boy dances up to her and for a while the two mirror one another, dancing back and forth, making faces and laughing at each other.

Then suddenly, she stops dancing long enough to pull me into the circle. Where is their justice? she wants to know. What have I done? Didn't I promise to be a Lola friend forever? I stand still. I listen. Wasn't I going to help them? The music booms loud into the space. The others continue dancing. But Lola Pilar is planted in the middle of that circle and she is confronting me. Where is their book? I let her shout at me, wave her arms at me. I have heard her song. I have danced with her. I have moved through protest crowds with her and stood for hours with nothing happening. I have been writing, but it is slow to come. I know that Lola Pilar has been to Japan multiple times to stand before the judges to ask these very questions. Her song is in her bones, the music too. And even when she is not fighting, she is fighting. Even though a hemp rope no longer binds her to those girls, she cannot break free.

Buhay ng "Comfort Woman"

Kay hirap ng buhay ng "comfort woman"
Tinitiis ang lahat ng kahirapan
Kay hirap ang aking pinagdaanan
Natutulog sa semento, walang banig na higaan

Ang buhay na aking tiniis
Sa kamay ng mga Hapones
Kay hirap ng buhay ng "comfort woman"
Nawawalan ng dignidad at karangalan

Ang buhay kung bakit ay ganito
Ang pait an sinapit na buhay ko
Kay hirap na buhay ng "comfort woman"
An sanhi ng karahasan, gawa ng digmaan

Ang dapat ating ipagsigawan
Itigil ang mg digmaan
Kay hirap sa mga kababaihan
Ang iba'y ginagahasa, ang iba'y pinapatay

Ang dapat ating ipagsigawan
Itigil ang mga digmaan
Kay hirap ng buhay ng "comfort woman"
Ang sanhi ng karahasan gawa ng digmaan

How the Lolas Raised the Roof

THE GIRLS PULL out their CDs and pop them into the machine. We've been dancing with the lolas all morning. Lola Prescila and Lola Pilar have been leading us across the concrete floor, cheek to cheek, teaching us the twists and turns of tango. I am a giant in their arms, stumbling to their quick, light steps. Absolutely ready to learn and heavy in my feet. I make them laugh and this is good. They make me feel a little off balance, a little out of sorts. This is good, too. Lolas Virgie, Remedios, and Ashang have been chasing all the girls about with their quick-quick-slow steps, making faces at each of us. Smiling. Sticking tongues out at us. Sometimes crossing their eyes. It is dance day. It is let-it-go day. The patio of Lolas' House is hot with our bodies' movement and the low fan hanging from the ceiling swirls lazily over us. All our lolas stand with us in the circle, giddy from the dance, waiting for the music to return.

Today the girls are dressed for American heat—the way I warned them not to do while in Manila. ("Cover up," I warned them; "dress modestly," I said. "No shorts. No tank tops. No sexy-sexy.") Tara has pulled her long bob up off her shoulders and fans herself as she collapses onto a plastic chair in her khaki shorts and baby blue camisole. Ana Fe flirts with the lolas, bending low to meet their faces, her eyes drawn into smiles so wide they're nearly shut. She has beautiful big arms and the face of a lion, and even without the music on she is still dancing with Lolas Remedios and Ashang. Neleh and Lizzie are hovering over their CDs, choosing just the right song. Today Lizzie has polished her tongue ring and put her hair into pin curls. She wears baggy overall long shorts over her tube top. Only Eliza sits alone in a corner, away from the lolas and the girls. She's staring off into space. Only Eliza has dressed the Filipino way, wearing long pants in the tropical heat, a modest T-shirt, and sneakers. Lately, she's been drifting away from us, dazed and unhappy with homesickness.

And then the music. Boom-boom. POP! Boom-boom. POP! Bass so loud the whole patio shakes. It is slow and heavy and methodical as heartbeat. It is rising from what seems to be the core of the house. It is hip-hop from the Americas. The lolas all jump up, ready to do their modern dance; the dalagas slide their bodies back into the circle. They raise their arms over their heads, palms flat to the sky like tribal dancers from the Cordillera. Their eyes go wide and their lips purse up. The shoulders pump up and down.

"Go Lola, go Lola! Get busy, go Lola!"

"Benita, Benita, get busy, Benita!"

Ana Fe leads Lola Benita, a lola once too lazy to dance, right into the middle of the circle.

"Get busy, Benita! Go, Lola, go Lola!"

Lola Benita puts her hand over her toothless mouth, smiling. She takes a step away from the center of the circle and the voices sing louder, "Go, Lola! Go, Lola!"

She shuts her eyes, the silver hair blows off her brown face, the hand reveals the smile—big, wide, empty. And then the shoulders twitch up. The arms rise. She wiggles her hips, stiff and awkwardly at first and then she rolls with it. The hands go up. The palms flatten to the ceiling above. She spins slowly around.

And next, a spill of laughter from all of us as we lift our hands, pump our shoulders to the beat, beat, beat . . . and the dalagas, the lolas, and I raise the roof. I, too, close my eyes and for a moment I am alone. It's as if our souls are rising right out of our bodies, spinning with the ceiling fan, rising up and up and out into the sky until we are gone from this space, from this earth, and we are dancing.

"Turtle! Turtle!"

WHENEVER A LOLA tells her story and she gets to the part where Japanese soldiers are barking orders at her, she assigns them the same line, over and over again: "Kura! Kura!" The words are curt. The words repeat. The voices are loud. "Kura! Kura!"

"Kura! Kura!" is the interruption between Now and Then. Now you are a carefree girl. You say prayers. You eat sweets. You have a family who loves you and calls you fat. Then you are Tira ng Hapones. Japanese leftovers. Damaged. Swollen. Raped. You can never go back to Now after Then.

"Kura! Kura!" is that moment when men clad in drab uniforms, boots, and steel-tipped bayonets march onto your farm, your rice paddy, your kitchen, and steal you. Rape you. Place you in a garrison with other girls and women. Make all of you into sex slaves.

"Kura! Kura!" is a made-up phrase. Not Tagalog. Not Japanese. Not one of the island dialects. It is the language of war. It is the command of the oppressor.

The stories come to you in bits and pieces. In words you understand. And some that are too deep. So malalim, not even your Tagalog-speaking mother knows their meaning. In the next eighteen years, you will read the way their bodies move. You will listen to their stories and some of it you will understand through words. You will get it in the way the voice swims through the air and touches you. Some of it you will hear and not know. Like this one. "Kura! Kura!" Use it in a sentence:

"I was doing laundry when I heard a noise. 'Kura! Kura!' said the soldiers as they held me by the hair. 'Kura! Kura!' they said, pushing me to the floor. And I knew that if I did not sit still, they would kill me."

When you search the Internet for a translation, you see images of turtles, not soldiers. You see an island resort. You see that in Indonesia the word does exist, but not the way the lolas use it.

BENITA ALIGANZA
Navotas, Metro Manila
May 7, 2002

Born June 27, 1930

Abducted by the Imperial Japanese Army,
1944, Tolosa Highway, Leyte

Little Good

THE SILVER VAN pulls up to the curb in front of Lola Benita's sari-sari store in Navotas. Sun blasts everywhere. Jars of candies, bins of rice, and bottles of orange drinks pop from behind the iron bars, and the shelves of her convenience store. Little boys hold their hands out as they order snacks through chicken wire. I leap out of the van and look into the storefront. Seeing Lilibeth, Lola's daughter, I sneak through the side entrance.

The sari-sari store is an enclosed counter with a window on the front steps of Lola Benita's house. Everything is cemented shut, and the sun has nowhere to enter. I must move through a dark maze to get to the sala. Nothing inside has changed. The house reminds me of a cave, smells of waste. I hold my breath. Television game shows blare, loud and bawdy, to a room cramped with furniture and children. Lilibeth calls over the contestants on *Game Ka Na Ba*, "May bisita, Ma!" And soon, Lola Benita shuffles in from the other side of the house. When she sees me she lights up.

"Hello, Lola!" I call out. "Kamusta?"

"Ito," she says. Like this.

Fluorescent lights shoot into dark spots, harsh and unnatural. But even in this light, I can see she looks good. Her face is relaxed and open. Her eyes are clear. She smiles and does not try to hide her missing teeth.

When I first met Lola Benita in 1999, she looked much older. Her face was always set in a frown. Her body was in constant pain. The girls and I would show up at Lolas' House and the lolas danced. Everybody danced. Everybody drew. Everybody acted. Everybody but Lola Benita.

Instead, she bent at the waist, hair falling in her eye, face scrunched up. "Ang tuhod ko," she said as she rubbed her knee. "Sakit. May arthritis ako."

The first couple of weeks, she watched us. The music pumped and thumped from the videoke speaker. The dalagas pulled all the women into a circle and we took turns shaking our booties. We raised our arms up and sang, "Go Lola, Go Lola! Get busy! Go Lola!" And each granny took her turn in the center of that circle, wiggling her body like she was twenty-two. Lola Benita watched us and by the end of the eight weeks, she was the one pulling us onto the dance floor, shoulders back and hips shifting.

But during her interview, she tapped at her chest and talked about the heaviness there. "Do I have to tell you my whole story?" she asked me.

"Of course not," I said.

"Do I have to tell it in order?"

"Tell it the way you remember it," I told her.

Then she took a breath, and she began:

When I went to school, my grandfather's house was used as the elementary school. At that time, we had heard about the Japanese. Then one day the planes came and bombed our place. I was helping my family plant corn in the field. We hid under the big trees. After the bombing, we continued to hide.

The Japanese went into our baranggay but they found none of us there. So what they did was they flew their planes and they dropped letters telling us if we didn't come to our houses they would burn everything. They would kill whomever they met. They turned my grandfather's house into a garrison. They captured our animals and butchered them. Now, the Filipinos were angry with the Japanese because of what they did to us. A certain Mr. Singco recruited the men and women to join the Philippine guerrilla movement. They armed themselves and one by one they killed the Japanese. The Japanese fought back.

I took the rice and ran through the kitchen. When I was outside, I heard, "Kura, kura!" A Japanese. Immediately I was taken like that, but I fought. I threw the rice. I resisted. They dragged me like that; they slapped me until my whole body was covered with bruises.

We ran for our lives and evacuated to a swamp area, along a small river on my mother's land. We stayed there for less than a month. However, we ran out of food. So I decided to get rice in our house because I knew we had plenty before the evacuation.

I was imprisoned in my own bedroom. When I woke up there were bruises all over my body. Didn't I struggle? I kicked the Japanese but he only stumbled. Then he took his pistol out and he did like that to me. I was imprisoned for one week. Every day they used me. During the night, I was used by many, one after the other. Eh, I could not fight. There was one good Japanese who took pity on me. Little good he did. He took a cloth and he tied it to me. After tying it like that, the bleeding stopped. I did not eat for days. Every day I was not given food and every day I was being used. I was twelve going on thirteen—what strength could I have to fight so many?

Since I was afraid the Japanese would see me, I passed through the fields and walked right into the house through the kitchen door. Then I went to the room where we kept the rice—I didn't know they were there—I should tell the whole story? I thought the Japanese were only at my grandfather's house. I didn't know.

Now my mother realized I had been captured. She got word to my father, who was a guerrilla. My father and two of my uncles decided to keep watch over the house. The Japanese patrolled the yard. There was an exchange of fire. Then my uncle came into the house and took me. I had no strength. I could not walk. My uncle carried me on his shoulder. We passed through the field we planted with corn.

She looked at me then, searching my face. "I told it out of order." I put my hand on hers and she said, "Tapos, pieces only. Kasi if I tell it all at once . . . I might be like that again. Noong araw nawala ako sa sarili ko."

Nawala ako sa sarili ko. At the age of twelve, Benita began a series of episodes during which she lost herself. I hear the lolas use this phrase a lot when they are talking about those moments, *I lost myself to myself. Nothing was I to myself.* Unlike other "comfort women" who were held in garrisons with other girls, she was the only one in her own house. Her body was not mature enough to endure the penetration of a man, much less several men. She said it was like going to sleep for a very long time. It was only during Liberation that she woke to the sounds of American guns. She woke to a body too weak to walk and covered in wounds. She woke to a ghost living inside her, making her afraid of all people. In 1992, when she heard Lola Rosa Henson on the radio, the spell was somehow broken. She stepped forward and released her story. She said telling her story lessened the pain in her chest, helped her to smile and to make friends.

Then, in June 1999, she came to Lolas' House, and she painted a little with the girls or sang a song. Once during a drama day, she and Ana Fe got so involved in their roles that they kicked their legs into the air and tumbled into the audience and laughed.

NINE YEARS LATER, I stand before her, and though I know she suffers from hypertension, she looks good. And then she tells me, "You know, you look just like a girl who used to come here. We loved her. She was tall like you and pretty like you. She used to make us laugh."

"Really, Lola?"

"She was American and she had girls with her. Students, I think."

I smile at her then. "Dalagas."

"Yes."

"Lola, look at me."

And then she takes my face in her hands and tilts it to the fluorescent bulb. She runs her palms across my check like she is reading my skin. "Yun pala!" she says, pinching me. "Evelina, it's you!"

And for a long time we stand in that dark entrance studying each other's faces—the eyes and the mouth, the ear lobes and the body, too. And that is how she comes to remember me—in bits and pieces, out of order and in many languages.

In front of Lola Benita's sari-sari store, also the entrance to her home
May 11, 2002

House on Bituan

Bituan Street, Baranggay Doña Imelda
Quezon City

GROWING UP IN Wisconsin, my siblings and I were outsiders, foreigners, even after my parents became naturalized citizens. We moved around seven times before my family settled down and built a house in Milwaukee. And even then, our family was the only Filipino family at my elementary school at Fairview South.

I grew up watching the kids around me spending weekends at their grandparents' houses. My best friend when I was eight was of Mexican descent and she was always at her nena's. Nena could cook.

All my grandparents lived in another country. I grew up hearing stories about them, longed for them, and delighted in the promise of their coming to America. When my father received an overseas call that his father had died at sixty-eight of a cardiac arrest, my dad's heartbreak sounded like a thousand mirrors shattering all at once. Watching him mourn my lolo's passing became the inspiration of my first serious short story, "Our Fathers." In that story, the protagonist obsesses over a sepia-toned photo of grandparents she has never met.

I REMEMBER WHEN my brother married my sister-in-law. I visited her family's summer house at the lake. I could feel the ghosts of all her grandmothers and grandfathers, all her aunts and uncles and all the other great-aunts and great-uncles who had summered in that house. It smelled old and musty and full of family stories. I was captivated by the thought of having such a space to call one's ancestral anything—summer cottage, home, getaway.

My sister-in-law's family was rooted to that land through that house,

74

by the lawns and the green grass and the trees. Her family has spent generations on that lake, in those waters.

We did not have an ancestral home in Wisconsin. Instead, I have Super-8 images, scrolling memories of my dad's parents in Macabebe (a room full of big people laughing with singsong voices), and of my mother's mother, Lola Clara Anca Lopez-Tan, a quiet and patient woman in a household of many adult children, dozens of happy apo, and their babysitters.

I had to fly halfway around the world to visit my ancestral bahay. I am in Lola Clara's house in Quezon City, and I have been trying to string the moments together like beads. I was small when I was here last, the youngest of five sets of cousins. My mother's father died in China when she was only two years old. When my lola was sick in the 1970s my mother was called to the Philippines. The rest of us were in school, and my dad had a busy medical practice, so Mom took my toddler brother with her. I have seen pictures of Lola sitting in a wheelchair in the driveway of Bituan, her hair piled high in a silver beehive and her cat-eye glasses sitting elegantly on her brown face. I've seen another photo, too, one of my mom and little brother next to Lola, who is under an oxygen tent. Just before my mother returned to the States, she went into Lola's bedroom to say goodbye and Lola pretended to be asleep.

Now I stand at the balcony and survey the lot. There used to be a green hill, and down at the bottom of the slope was a little grotto to Mama Mary. She was blue and white and had her own cave of stones surrounding her. My cousin Gilbert and I used to chase each other around that lawn, and I have this sensation of rolling down the hill to land at the very feet of the Mother of God.

In the corner where the grotto used to be stands my aunt's greenhouse. The hill has been leveled and Mama Mary has been placed on a shelf in the stone wall of the new garden.

Here is where Gilbert gave me a scar on the arm. Gilbert was a biter and the whole family remembers the time he bit my cheek, but it was my arm. He has the story: I had a truck, he told me. He wanted that truck and he demanded I hand it over. I would not. He insisted. I would not. He grabbed my arm and sunk his teeth into it. I cried out. Uncle Doming—a big man with a belly and a loud voice—came out of the house. He was Gilbert's uncle, too, but he treated us like his kids because that is the Filipino way. Gilbert says that Uncle spanked him. Told him not to hurt his cousin like that again. But somehow, I think he did bite me again. Anyway, he used to call me Apple Cheeks.

It is my lola, Clara Anca Lopez-Tan, whom I don't remember vividly. It is my lola whom I am dying to know but cannot hear or see. She appears in the pictures, always at the center of the photographs, always the matriarch—a petite, brown-skinned woman with her hair pulled back into a silver bun. Her earlobes hung heavy with diamond earrings. She had a belly—not so big, but a belly nonetheless.

When I was two and three years old, all the aunts and uncles and their children would meet here on Sundays. We spent all day playing in Lola's garden. I remember dangling my feet in a lily-pad pond with giant goldfish swimming in constant circles. We ate big lunches and the uncles played poker until sunset. The aunties broke into groups of four and rolled mah-jongg tiles. Or they joined the kids when the ya-yas, our babysitters, laid us down for a nap. We'd wake ready for our merienda, afternoon sweets and cakes we nibbled as the cook readied a feast for our big family. My lola watched over us like a guardian angel. Like a queen.

I CLOSE MY eyes and try to hear her voice, and I cannot. My brother says that when he was living here as a medical student, he'd fall asleep studying in her bedroom and that there were nights he'd feel her close to him, waking him up, telling him to study. I imagine her talking to us as babies, holding us, feeding us, and nothing comes up. I knew my lola and yet she appears like a phantom in my memories.

Uncle says the house was a bungalow back then. One floor with rooms where different families lived. Auntie Goring, Uncle Ente, and Gilbert in one room. My then-bachelor Uncle Romy in another. In the back, my Uncle Doming and his family built another house. When my parents and I arrived the house was too crowded, so my parents rented the house on the corner of the street. My parents had two sons while we lived in that house. These days I drive past the house and I try to see through the blue gate, over the high walls.

The bungalow is gone. Everything has been renovated and the first floor has an open concept—with a marble floor stretching from living room to dining room to the door that leads to the kitchen. There is both a dirty kitchen and a beautiful Western kitchen, complete with granite counters. I wander the hallways and the garden and I am silent. I am looking for that thing that is so familiar to me.

Doesn't every kid have a lola's house, a granny who spoiled them and fed them too many sweets? Why can't I remember her?

MY GRANDMOTHER WAS a thirty-six-year-old widow with seven children when World War II broke out. My mother and her sister Josefa are about the age of the lolas, so they were twelve and seventeen when the Japanese bombed Pearl Harbor. Lolo was a successful Chinese businessman, and he left my grandmother a coconut plantation. Back then, they did not live here in the city but in the provinces, in the town of Macalelon. That house was bigger than this one. That house was made of narra wood and had a staircase, wide and steep. At the top of the steps were two elegant portraits of my grandparents. The windows were made not of glass but of capiz shell. That was the house that my mother grew up in, and when the war broke out, my grandmother took her children and went into hiding. They say my mother looked Japanese, so when the family traveled on trains, her older sisters covered her face. She was only twelve but already well read and bookish.

I have always wanted to return to the Philippines with my parents, to travel the roads with them and to see the houses we called home. Every time I return, I visit my elders. I look for evidence of our past lives. I wonder at the way my family's lives turned out so different from those of the lolas I'm interviewing.

A LONG TIME ago, my uncle woke up in the middle of the night as a clock drifted by his bed, then a radio, a cup, and a saucer. Even the chairs danced around, bumping doorways and walls, bobbing about like ships lost at sea. It was the rainy season and the waters had entered the house and rose up high. My grandmother climbed aboard the piano with her legs to the side like she was sitting on a blanket in the park. She pointed to items with her fan, telling everyone to fetch them before they floated out to sea. But even in this image, Lola is a portrait, not a Super-8 memory, not a video, and certainly not three-dimensional.

I admit it. I want her to show herself. To appear in the middle of the garden like a beautiful saint. I want her to tap me on the shoulder in the middle of the night and point me to my destiny. It will take me another few years and a move to Miami to see her dancing along the green boulevards of Kendall, her white hair finally free from the silver bun, and her clothing loose like angel wear.

So coming home to Bituan, where I first learned to walk, where I began using words to connect to other people, and where my first language was neither English nor Tagalog but a mixed bag of Tagalog, English, and Kapampangan, I am mesmerized. I want to see ghosts. I want to know that this is where we come from. Where I came from. And it is where I'm going.

CRISTITA ALCOBER

Born July 26, 1926, Barrio Cogon,
San Jose, Tacloban City, Leyte

Abducted by the Imperial
Japanese Army, 1942,
San Jose, Tacloban City, Leyte

Filed Postwar Compensation Suit,
April 2, 1993, Tokyo District Court

Ocean of Umiyak

IT IS AN integration day and my five students and I are scattered all over Antipolo, each of us hanging out with a different survivor. Eliza has been assigned to Lola Cristita Alcober. Eliza is native-born Pinay, having left Manila when she was twelve, fluent, and longing to come back home. While I am at Lola Flora Banton's bedside, Eliza is on the other side of town, following Lola Cristita around the empty concrete kitchen, fetching bowls and mixing pots, pouring juice, and setting her table in total silence. The two converse in one-word sentences, glancing now and then at each other, acting just like grandmother and grandchild, when suddenly Lola Cristita stands up and tells her, "Sandali," and, commanding her to hold on, leaves the house and runs her way through all of Antipolo to find me.

Lola Cristita walks right into Lola Flora Banton's house and pulls me out into the sunshine, dragging me through the street. I think something has gone wrong and so together, we climb up rubble-shattered roads and down dirt-path alleys. She doesn't say much, doesn't answer me when I ask, "Saan ba tayo, Lola?" Still pulling my arm, she points with her free hand to her two-story cement-block house. "Sa bahay ko," she says.

Reaching her house, we barrel through the doorway and hike up the steps. And when we get to the top, I see Eliza and Maribel, the LILA Pilipina organizer, sitting quietly at a table. "What's wrong?" I ask.

"She just got up in the middle of the meal," Eliza says. "She didn't say why."

"Kuripot sila," Lola Cristita says. "Gugutumin siya."

"Hindi, La. Talagang walang pera sila. The Bantons are really poor," Maribel says. Then to me Maribel says, "She was afraid they wouldn't feed you."

"I ate," I say as Lola Cristita ushers me into a seat and Eliza puts a plate before me. Fish soup and rice. The fish eye floats in a broth of tomato and onions, in a sea of wilted kang kong, watching me, reminding me that it is my duty to eat. I have my second serving of sinigang, but this time in the house of Lola Cristita. As soon as I am done eating, she gestures me to follow her up another set of stairs.

Lola Cristita Alcober is short and round—round little head and round belly and two round breasts. Everything moves her. When the women of Lolas' House sing and dance, she cries. When women quarrel over little things, she cries. When a lola gives her testimony, she cries. When visitors arrive for the first time, she cries. She cries when you listen and when you pull her to the dance floor. She breaks into tears and sobs, kissing your face when you are leaving. Everything moves her and we all call her Lola Iyak-Iyak. Lola Cry-Cry.

Out on the balcony she talks fast, and when all I do is listen, she tugs on my arm and points at my camera. The Dalaga Project has been in Manila only a week and we are just getting to know the women. Formal interviews are so cold and intrusive. We have made a choice not to conduct them at all. Instead, we hold days like integration day, visiting the lolas' homes and seeing their lives firsthand. Our days with them are meant to build friendships respectfully through dancing and singing and art making. But here we are standing in the beautiful afternoon light of Lola Cristita's cement balcony surrounded by palm trees, ferns, and other lush greenery, on the verge of an interview. She insists I turn on my camera.

"She wants to tell you her story," Maribel tells us. "She wants you to tape her."

"Now?" I look at Lola Cristita, at the very center of her graying eye, and there it is, the first sign of a tear. She smiles at me then. I look over my shoulder to Eliza, who is just behind me. Eliza nods, says nothing. "Sige, i on mo na," Lola Cristita coaches me, "I tape mo na."

I obey. I flip the screen open and nudge the switch. The light flashes green and the mini monitor lights up blue and then her face emerges, an apparition on the tiny screen. I hit the record button. I pull back and she begins in a calm way. She gives her testimony slowly and in Tagalog.

> Ako si Cristita Alcober. When I was a teenager I lived in Samar. My mother came from there. My father was from Tacloban. My father sold tobacco and he used to travel. My parents met in Dumaraga. He courted my mother until they were married. My mother was already orphaned. My father still had a mother and they lived in Dumaraga. All three of us were born there in Dumaraga. I was born on July 26, 1926.

I zoom the camera in tight on her face. The golden sunlight reveals all the lines on her skin, sometimes drifting to her silver hair tucked behind a thick earlobe. The voice is soft and rough like a dirt road scattered with fine pebbles. Her words float out slowly. I hold the camera with my hand and I watch her, not the viewfinder. She smiles as she talks. She wraps her arms around herself—the right arm reaching up across her chest to the left shoulder and the other cinched around her waist. Now and then the hand on her shoulder goes up to gesture at the camera.

> One day my mother told me and my fourteen-year-old brother to go to Barrio Cogon to buy fish. At that time, I was sixteen years old. We started walking at eight in the morning and returned the following day. We had to walk because there was no other transportation. The Japanese were staying at the San Jose airport near the white beach. We walked. We looked like children. Even though I was sixteen, I looked like a small child. I could walk without clothes and they would think I was a child.
> When we arrived home, my mother was no longer in the house. The Japanese were already there. We were caught and held by the Japanese. We were afraid and we were crying. We were afraid they would kill us, so even if they kicked us, we didn't mind. The soldiers forced us to walk toward San Jose airport. My brother and I held hands.

As Lola Cristita speaks, her breath goes short. Her words falter and then suddenly she is speaking quickly, no longer in Tagalog, the language we understand, but Visayan. Maribel does her best to interpret Lola's dialect but only because she knows Lola's testimony.

Eliza and I step closer to her, the camera shooting her mouth, her eye, the inside of her ear. Eliza and I exchange glances. We have tears streaming down our faces.

And this is where we lose her. The deeper she goes into her experience, the further away she seems, lost somewhere on the island of Leyte, in the center of its green wilderness. She hiccups. Her eyes gloss over. The words tilt left and right. Grow harder to decipher. She paws at her collarbone and winces. Slips back and forth between Tagalog and Visayan, and even though we cannot not understand her, we find ourselves slipping into the past, feeling the weight of the experience. We enter the small house in Cogon only to find the Japanese soldiers waiting for us, swooping down on us, dragging us down the road. It is in her eyes. It is in the lapses of her breath. Eliza and I, like brother and sister, are torn apart, one made to turn left and the other forced right and the heart raw like meat ripped in two. The tears wash Lola Cristita's face and her breathing grows shallow, but she does not stop talking. We are at the airstrip by the water. She keeps talking. We are in a pit of sand dug for fish. We are thirty girls thrown together, like catches of the day, imprisoned by barbed-wire walls and bamboo-locked doors. She talks over her own crying now. Faster and louder and now she is going into Waray, a native language so deep and so intense that it has to be coming from her very core.

On this day, she tells me everything, mixing all her words together like a giant batch of alphabet soup, the Waray and Tagalog and Visayan, the occasional English word tossed in for flavor, all holding their shape, translating her two years in that fish bin, drowning with thirty other girls. She tells me all I need to know, though I understand nothing but the tears rolling down my own face.

Quezon City
January 2002

WHEN I RETURN three years later, Lola Cristita is sitting at Lolas' House with the other women, watching me kiss each lola on the cheek. She waits for me to work my way around the patio as the women grab my arms and my neck, pinch my cheeks, and tickle my waist. She waits as some of them holler my name. And when I get to her, she lets me reach to pull her up. Smiling, she looks away from me, but the tears are already falling. "Lola Iyak-Iyak, kamusta ka?" And when I reach down to kiss her cheek, she sniffs my skin

"I hear you are taking some of the lolas home."

"With me?" I ask her. "To America?"

She pinches me and says, "No, to our provinces."

Sa probinsya. Yes. Excursion tours to their sites of abduction and to their former garrisons.

"You bring me."

"There are beaches there, no?"

She nods.

"Okay, La, if you promise to go swimming with me."

"Sige," she answers.

"If you wear a bikini, too."

"Okay," she says in English laughing and pinching my arm. "Bikini na tayo."

And every time after that, she asks me when we're going to go, and I ask her about the bikini, and she laughs and says, "Oo nga. Sabi ko na, I'll wear one."

Tacloban
May 14, 2002

LOLA CRISTITA, LILA Pilipina organizer Sol Rapisura, and I take a little plane from Manila on the island of Luzon to the Visayan island of Leyte. The plane is small and feels every current, moves on the shift of a cloud and the breath of our pilot. Lola Cristita smiles, looking out the window from behind a pair of movie-star sunglasses. She points as though she can see her house, floating in a sea of trees, set in the middle of an island in the vast Pacific Ocean. She is going to make us taste the local cuisine and drink tuba, moonshine, fermented coconut water.

When the plane lands, she stands before anyone has had a chance to unbuckle her belt. Lola Cristita wiggles her hips down the aisle of the narrow plane, and stepping onto the tarmac she motions to us to hurry up and follow.

If this were Manila, she would wait for us, but in Tacloban she leads the way down streets like the mayor, calling out to passersby and waving. Dirt roads, wide and lazy, lead to a smattering of houses, sari-sari stores, and vegetable stands. We walk past a church, maybe a school. Occasionally, a motor trike zooms past us and kicks up the dust. The trees tower over us. Green and thick, they shade us, tell us how old they and this town are.

We are finding our way to the house where she grew up. We visit distant relations. "I'm back," she tells them in Visayan, "I brought my friends." Her words float by me like people on the street. Some of them I recognize. Tagalog words. Sometimes English. Some are variations of words from her testimony, and others are foreign and awkward to my ear. We stop at a house and Lola raps on a screen. A woman swings a door open. Lola Cristita greets her, her hands gesturing north and south and her smile widening with each word. The woman listens and then nods. She speaks back quickly and calls a name or two, says that one married, that one moved away. Somebody died. And after a while, Lola Cristita points to the side of a house, at a porch made of bamboo with plastic chairs that line the walls.

"We go that way," she tells us.

Her voice rises above the cock's crow. She pushes her sunglasses up her flat nose, her gold rings and bracelets shimmering in the sun. I trail behind her, the camera lens zoomed out, shooting the sleepy barrio. I focus on her gait, how quick and certain, how fast. This is not the same Lola Cristita as in Manila. That woman is always tired. I smile to see her like this.

As we move toward the location of her house, the nipa huts and small structures grow scarce and the grasses spike past her shoulders, the trees shooting up into the blue sky, limbs bowing toward us like angel wings.

This was the walk she and her brother Marianito took on the way home from the market that day. These old paths existed in some form when the trees were not so tall and leafy. But the grasses must have been this high, I think, the shrubbery this fat. The crickets singing and leaping to the skies just like this. The silence of the countryside and the heat of the sun feel old and familiar to the skin. It must have been like this, I think, watching her.

We walk past a porch and as we turn the corner a little woman with white hair and a long walking stick comes out, calling to us in Waray. She is at least ninety years old. The two old women have never met, but they stop and talk like longtime neighbors trading tsismis. But this is not gossip. They are exchanging war stories.

The old woman is not surprised by Lola Cristita's experience. She knows. It was what happened back then, but no one ever talked about it. She wishes us well and watches us walk away, blessing us as we go.

On the path, we run into another woman, small like Lola Cristita, but dark with a long low ponytail. Lola Cristita grabs the lady's arm and starts talking at her. The woman doesn't recognize her at first, but then a flurry of arms goes up. They were girlhood friends, I am told. They knew each other when the war broke out.

And slowly, I begin to figure out that every person Lola Cristita meets, whether it is someone from her past or a stranger whom she has stopped for directions, every person is hearing her testimony.

"I never knew," says her friend. "I never heard," she tells me.

"And how do you feel now that you know?" I ask.

"I want to cry," she tells me in Visayan, "I am sad."

More than fifty years of silence and suddenly we float down the rural roads leading out of Tacloban and she calls out her truth like a herald from God.

In the moment, I cannot understand their words. I can feel it. The way the women listen to her, the way they stand so close to her and never move away. I see it in the eyes. There is a matter-of-fact way about all of them, the storyteller and the listener. So these stories are true, then, the women say; I've heard these things, but no one ever really told the story before. The story was in the trees, in the grasses, integrated in the sands on the beaches, but never spoken out loud.

Her childhood friend joins us as we walk to where the house once stood. We climb through tall grasses and I almost lose Lola Cristita in the brush. I follow the glint of her white halo.

Sol is just behind her, and looking beyond Lola she calls out, "Lola, dahan dahan! May asa!"

"A snake?" I yell back, "Lola, stop!"

But her fat arms strike at the tall grasses, and she is yelling out, "My house was here! This is the place!"

"Lola! May asa dijan!"

She doesn't care. She stomps through the grass until she reaches a clearing. We are in the countryside now, and there is nothing but beautiful green around us broken up with the occasional stalk of a tall, skinny palm tree. It is the way I imagine Paradise, a landscape touched by God, fertile, lush, and out of control. Behind Lola Cristita is the black skeleton of a nipa hut, burnt by the sun. She stands in the middle of the clearing and tells me to turn the camera on, brushing down her skirt and adjusting her white kimona blouse.

"Sandali, po," I tell her, snapping the zoom tight to the fine lines of her skin then widening to cover the whole landscape. The shot reveals how small she is, how brown and out of place she is, lost in a field of green grass.

Her voice rises from this space and her words, Tagalog words, float like smoke filling the air.

> Here. We lived here—my mother, two younger brothers, and a sister. My mother sent my father away to live with his mistress in Manila. He had many. My mother was a quiet woman. She didn't have time for his fooling around. She was focused on raising us. She made a life of washing people's dirty laundry.
>
> By 1942, the Japanese had landed in Leyte. They set up a garrison on the white beaches near the airport. There were rumors that they wandered about San Jose, bullying the natives.

Lola Cristita sings, raspy but strong, sings as she gestures the story with her arms, pointing in the direction of San Jose. The trees and grasses have grown still. Sol has stopped moving behind me. Only her girlhood friend moves around, sometimes stepping into the frame of the lens, sometimes sighing audibly.

> One day my mother sent me and my younger brother Marianito to Cogon to buy fish and matches and other household sundries. Because there were no cars, we had to wake up early and set off at eight in the morning, walking the six kilometers to Cogon. I was sixteen, but I was small like a child and girls like myself were not interested in men the way girls are now. I was a child

obeying my mother. And at that time, I was ugly, I was not beautiful like now.

When we returned we found Japanese soldiers waiting at our house.

How can we fight them? We were children!

They smelled bad and they were dirty in their soiled brown uniforms and heavy combat boots. They dragged my brother and me out of the house and down the road and all I could think was, Where is my mother? Where are my brother and sister?

She turns to look at the empty hut, at the hollow bamboo fence and the thick thatched roof. Here, she slips into Visayan, leaving the Tagalog there in the grass. Here the words shatter the calm. She does not stop. Indecipherable and blue, her syllables fall like seeds, sinking deep into the earth.

Site of Lola Cristita's home before World War II
Barrio Cogon, San Jose, Tacloban City, Leyte
May 14, 2002

LATER THAT DAY we climb into our rented car and drive the path she and her brother walked to the airstrip in Cogon. I imagine the way soldiers pushed them along, kicking them when they faltered or butting them with the heel of their rifles when they moved too slowly. For us, the six-kilometer drive is quick, but for Lola Cristita and her brother the walk must have been interminable.

We get to the airstrip, and the sun shines everywhere. The gentle tide laps at the shore and the white sands glisten. The planes have long stopped landing and the sea hushes everything still. Palm fronds whisper.

Not yet out of the car and her tears are falling. I tell her we don't have to do this, but she pushes her pawlike hand past my shoulder and climbs out of the car, waving us to follow her, to come.

Once my brother and I reached the airport, we were separated and I never saw him again. The soldiers brought me to the "comfort station" by the sea. It was a cage fishermen made for their fish. A tin roof and barbed-wire walls shaped like a hut. The floor was nothing but white sands. The soldiers tossed me into the jail. How many girls? Maybe thirty women and girls. I didn't know them.

I stand before the sandpit, eight to ten feet in diameter, under the shade of coconut and banana trees.

"This is where they kept us," she says. Lola Cristita wipes the corner of her eye with a tissue I've handed her. "All of us here, like animals."

"This was a fish bin?" I ask.

"During the war," she tells me.

I picture the women trapped in a cage, their arms and legs pressed against their torsos, their tears flowing everywhere. "How did you fit?" I ask. The sand pit is a few hundred yards from the sea, set on a thick lawn of grass, no different than a garden gazebo.

"I was the youngest," she tells me. "I was sixteen and only three others—Natty, Gunyan, and Tila—spoke Waray. I had no one else to talk to."

Lola Cristita describes the Japanese soldiers and their rifles guarding the hut, circling like sharks. "Since there was no bathroom, we had to wash ourselves there," she says, pointing to the sea. "And they were always watching."

Each morning the men would make us count off. During the day, we dug foxholes. We'd cover the bottom of the pits with banana leaves and then line the foxhole with sandbags. I thought they would shoot us right there. I thought we were digging our graves. The Japanese forced us to work from sunrise to dusk. Hardly anything to eat. Only small portions of rice and beans. I was always hungry and thirsty and feeling weak.

Her voice breaks up, like a radio wave going in and out of frequency. She refuses to stop and wipe her nose, to swallow or to spit. Instead, the words rise up and out of her, broken up and spinning everywhere. The wind blows our hair about and the tide hits the shore like a child in the midst of a tantrum. Even the ocean remembers.

On my third night, the Japanese reached into the bin and pulled all thirty of us out. They yanked me by my hair and pulled me by my leg and threw me and the girls under the trees. There at the edge of the water more than fifty soldiers raped us. You know, I could see the stars. I could feel the black sky coming down as if to suffocate me. I could not bear it. At first I resisted and the soldier slapped me hard, pushed me to the ground, and broke my left collarbone. You see? Irritated, he raised his bayonet and stabbed me in the groin, and then, not taking time to wipe the blood away, he raped me again, even with this open wound. He was the first soldier that night. And then another climbed on top of me and put himself inside me. And then another man. And then another. This went on all night and did not stop until six the next morning, just as the sun started to show. Just as we were told to file for roll call and another day of foxhole digging.

Nobody noticed my broken collarbone. Nobody cared that my groin was bleeding and swollen. Nobody noticed the open wound oozing. I could not sit, or stand, or lie still without wincing from pain, and nobody noticed. That next morning, I joined my companions and I dug foxholes like nothing was wrong.

> For the next two years, I was raped by as many as ten soldiers
> a night. Japanese soldiers from other camps arrived. Long lines
> of men, waiting. In the dark, I could hear the women around
> me—some struggling, gasping, and crying out—others cry-
> ing like me. Sometimes there was the sound of a blade slicing
> through the body or a shot of a gun and then silence. So I would
> lie on the ground too scared to resist them.
>
> They were dogs. Some of them were circumcised, others were
> not. All of them were dogs.

I look at her and try to picture a sixteen-year-old with a child's slight body—no breasts, no hips, just arms and legs and a thin torso bearing the weight of ten men a night. I can feel the tears welling up inside me, but I refuse to let them fall. I focus on her face now. I focus on her body. Back then, it must have been a strong body not to shatter into pieces. Now she is fat and full of curves, but then, she was a child. Her left shoulder sits crooked on top of her frame. "Even during my period," she tells me, tears falling and falling everywhere, "they forced me to serve their sexual needs. They told me to wipe away the menstrual flow with my only dress, then raped me without mercy."

Today the sun is so hot and the water crashes everywhere. I hand my camera to Sol and I walk over to Lola Cristita to hold her body as it shakes, as the tears fall out of her and her story fills the landscape. I cannot hold all of her, though my arms are long enough to wrap around her twice. She is shaking and her words come out in fragments, broken syllables of glass, cutting at the air, pushing against my own body, then sinking into me and settling at my core.

"I never saw my brother," she says. "He died of dehydration. And all I could think about was seeing my mother."

"Okay, Lola," I whisper, "calm now, Lola, calm down."

But she won't quiet down. It is too late. "At the time, the sight of a Japanese cap, a uniform, or a pair of pants would strike terror in me." The soldiers would come to the hut, bayonets held up high and threaten them all. They'd say, "Okay suksok? Patay ka!"

Okay, suksok. Just like it sounds. Suksok. The interminable sound of rape. Of sex without consent. Okay to have sex with you? And then the pause, the space between the command where her imagined re-

sponse would fall. And then an answer to her silence—(if not) patay
ka. Or you're dead.

"I wanted to escape," she tells me, "but how when the guards are always there? I wanted to kill myself, but how?"

When the Americans arrived, we were able to escape. I was very
ashamed. By then, I had been a prisoner for more than a year.
The Japanese evacuated, but there were still some there. All of
us were able to escape.

The fish house had a floor made of sand and that was where
we slept. The Americans flew in on many airplanes and jets.
They shot at the coconuts. The planes flew so low they were
lower than the coconut trees. We were so afraid of the bombs
falling. And then, the girls and I found a way to cut the barbed-
wire fence and we slowly stepped on the wires until they were
down. We ran as fast as we could. The Japanese did not stop us
because of all the planes flying so low. We found out later they
were the U.S. Air Force.

Once the fence was down, we ran in all directions. We didn't
know which way to go, but I ran in the direction of Tacloban.
When I got there, I could not locate my mother. I went to a store
and saw someone I knew, Gina. I stayed with her and sold tomatoes in the market until I heard my mother was living in a quar-
ry. So I went to look for her. When I found her, she and I rented
a place where my older sister, my mother, and I could live.

In 1945, I met a man and we were planning to get married.
I was pregnant five months when he found out I was raped by
the Japanese soldiers. He didn't understand. He left me without a word. When my son was seventeen he went to Manila and
I followed him there. That's where I met my second husband,
Jesus. We have not been blessed with children because I was old
when we married. I was thirty-five and he was twenty-five. I was
ashamed to marry him, so we just lived together.

Lola Rosa says when she came forward she felt different.
That's what I wanted too—to feel different, but how? It's different if it was just one Japanese raping me, but there were so
many. I felt ashamed.

I ask her if coming forward helped.

Nabawas-bawasan ang dibdib ko. Nabawas-bawasan an hirap. My heart felt lighter. My trouble grew smaller.

I imagine the ocean in the middle of a storm. The skies are black. Waves pitch high to the clouds. Then a child's beach bucket dips into the ocean, pulls out a pail full of water. Cristita tells the story again and the bucket sinks back into the angry waves, pulls out another quart, maybe a gallon and every time she tells the story, bawas-bawasan. Little by little she is relieved. Little by little the pain shifts. The burden lightens. But never all the way.

Sometimes, when she is at Lolas' House and the women are dancing or laughing, when the women are loading onto a jeepney on their way to a rally at the Japanese embassy, it is as if there is a slow leak at the bottom of the ocean and all the pain is draining from her, but then she remembers, and the tears start up. "I am quiet," she tells me, "I am remembering."

**Miami, Florida
June 2011**

SINCE SHE PASSED away, I see her in my dreams. Her words fill the spaces in my heart. Some flow right through me, some move like stones and wedge between my shoulder blades, blocking the flow of all my energy. I have been trying to rid myself of all these words. Trying to write them down as fast as I can, but sometimes I feel so fatigued. So uneasy. In my dreams she is smiling at me, looking at me as if she hasn't seen me in years. But you are always with me, I think. And then I ask her, how are you?

And she says, good, waiting.

I say, what are you waiting for?

For you to write the story.

I'm trying, I tell her. Are you still crying?

Sometimes.

Still?

Not for me, for the world. We need to tell the story so the Japanese can heal. So everyone can heal.

And in my dream, the ocean evaporates like rain and the wind dies down and somewhere, there is an island where Cristita has reclaimed her beautiful child body and she has donned a two-piece swimsuit and she is dancing, hands up in the air, head thrown back, song rising to the sky.

I Have Returned

Fulbright Senior Research Scholar
December 2001–August 2002

WHEN I RETURN, I take eight months to interview thirteen lolas. By now two of the original lolas—Lola Lucia Alvarez and Lola Catalina Lorenzo—have died. Instead of taking their testimonies all in one day, I spread each interview across the calendar. And I take my time. I spend half days, whole days, and socials with each of the surviving lolas. I travel with seven of the lolas around the archipelago to visit their hometowns. I join them at rallies, and I sit with them during their organizational meetings. This time I don't just let them talk. We are more familiar with one another. We have built friendships and family ties. I have thirteen grandmothers. My own lolas—Lola Kula and Lola Clara—have long since died, and I never had a chance to spend much time with them. So I make believe these lolas are my lolas. And they take me on as if I am their own. I ask them questions. Hard ones. Paano yan Lola? I want to know the details of their accounts—how had they been raped. Ilan sila? *How many*? Ilan beses? *How many times*? Araw-araw? Sometimes I ask the questions more than once and in different ways. Sometimes Lola ignores my questions, not because she doesn't understand. Sometimes she doesn't want to answer. Mostly I want to know how what happened then affects their lives now. Paano, La? Each lola answers the same questions in her own way.

When Ana Fe and I first interviewed the women in 1999, we were naïve and we sat in a room for fourteen hours taking each woman's testimony. We were wrecks at the end of the day. Our eyes were swollen from crying. My nose was so stuffed I could barely breathe. Lola Regina told the other girls, "The stories have entered their bodies."

At the time, I thought it was a poetic phrase. I had no idea she meant it. Since then, I cannot seem to sit still. Something drives me to come back, to stay on it, to be the dutiful daughter, but this time, I tell myself, I will protect myself. I will stay balanced. I will not let the stories take over the way they did last time.

At the end of the day, when I call it a wrap, I do just that. I fold up my tripod and break down the camera. I kiss and hug each lola goodbye and I wave to them. On my way home to St. Scholastica's, my driver, Bong, and I talk about the day. How the lola had reacted to retelling her life, or how the story itself was special and remarkable in its own way. This time I am prepared and I don't let myself cry. Not once.

At the end of the days, I go to the gym. I practice yoga and I sweat. I spend weekends with my very large extended family.

I do my best to take care of myself so that the lolas' stories will not drown me or send me into despair. Every morning, I read spiritual texts. Every Wednesday night Sister Mary John Mananza, my host at St. Scholastica's, takes me to a meditation center in Makati and I chant and meditate. On Sundays I visit a circuit of Catholic churches with my cousins and aunties and uncles and I pray. Because I am a contemporary Pinay from America, I practice healthy living. I stop eating meat all together. I think I will be fine.

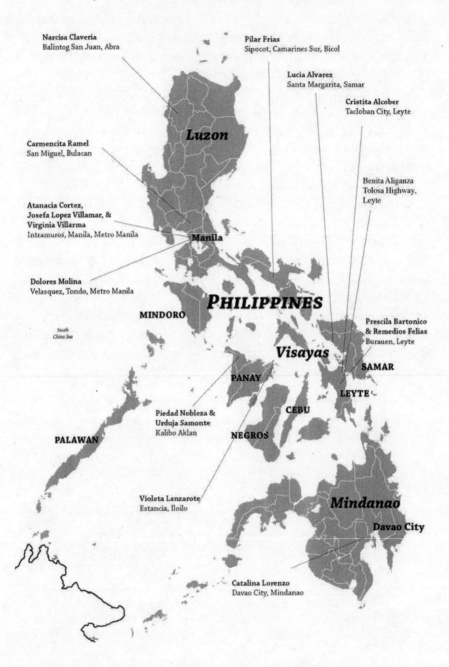

Narcisa Claveria
Balintog San Juan, Abra

Pilar Frias
Sipocot, Camarines Sur, Bicol

Lucia Alvarez
Santa Margarita, Samar

Cristita Alcober
Tacloban City, Leyte

Luzon

Carmencita Ramel
San Miguel, Bulacan

Benita Aliganza
Tolosa Highway,
Leyte

**Atanacia Cortez,
Josefa Lopez Villamar, &
Virginia Villarma**
Intramuros, Manila, Metro Manila

Manila

Dolores Molina
Velasquez, Tondo, Metro Manila

PHILIPPINES

MINDORO

South
China Sea

Visayas

**Prescila Bartonico
& Remedios Felias**
Burauen, Leyte

SAMAR

PANAY

LEYTE

**Piedad Nobleza &
Urduja Samonte**
Kalibo Aklan

CEBU

PALAWAN

NEGROS

Mindanao

Violeta Lanzarote
Estancia, Iloilo

Davao City

Catalina Lorenzo
Davao City, Mindanao

Lolas' Sites of Abduction by the Imperial Japanese Army

*Funded by Fulbright Philippine American Education Foundation,
January–August 2002*

DATE	NAME	LOCATION
Feb. 18–19	Cristita Alcober	Antipolo
Feb. 21	Narcisa Claveria	Manila
Feb. 26–28	Pilar Frias	Antipolo
Mar. 10–11	Urduja Samonte	Manila
Mar. 18–19	Atanacia Cortez	Manila Fort Santiago
Apr. 22–23	Prescila Bartonico	Navotas
Apr. 25	Piedad Nobleza	Navotas
Apr. 29	Josefa Lopez Villamar	Navotas
Apr. 30	Dolores Molina	Navotas
May 2	Josefa Lopez Villamar	Intramuros San Augustine Church
	Dolores Molina	Velasquez Tondo, Manila
May 10–11	Benita Aliganza	Navotas
May 14–18	Cristita Alcober	Tacloban
May 21–26	Piedad Nobleza	Aklan, Kalibo
Jun. 4–5	Violeta Lanzarote	Manila
Jun. 6–7	Virginia Villarma	Navotas Del Pan, Tondo, Manila
Jun. 8–10	Narcisa Claveria	Balintog, San Juan, Abra
Jun. 14	Carmencita Ramel	San Miguel Bulacan

NARCISA ADRIATICO CLAVERIA

Born December 23, 1931,
Balintog, San Juan, Abra

Abducted by the Imperial
Japanese Army, 1943,
Balintog, San Juan, Abra

Filed Postwar Compensation Suit,
September 1993, Tokyo District Court

Ilocana Street Warrior, after Gabriela Silang

Philippine State of the Nation Address Protest
Epifanio de los Santos Avenue
July 26, 1999

WHEN I FIRST see Narcisa Claveria, she is standing on the curb at a protest rally, holding a bullhorn to her mouth. Her hand waves at the sky and her legs move to the cadence of her speech:

> I was among the youngest of eight children. In 1943, when I was twelve years old, my father was the barrio's baranggay captain. A battalion from the Imperial Japanese Army invaded our village. The soldiers went all over the barrio. They were searching for insurgents and guerrillas. They invaded all our homes and questioned our villagers. They found almost all the residents of each household except one, and this house was the house believed to be the house of Filipino guerrillas. Soldiers barged into our house and confronted my father. As baranggay captain, he was responsible for the whereabouts of all the citizens in Balintog, San Juan, Abra. Where were these people, they asked him.
>
> My father told them he didn't know. Maybe they were fishing at the river, or maybe they were at work. "If you're responsible for this village," the Japanese demanded, "why don't you know where they are?" The soldiers accused my father of hiding them.

Then he persuaded the Japanese to give him an hour to locate them. "I'll find them," he said. "You'll see."

Traveling from Metro Manila to San Juan, Abra
June 8, 2002

WE LEAVE MANILA—streets lined with miles of idling motors, with people darting, dodging, pushing past vendors, beggars, and stalled motor trikes, with garbage-stacked alleys and shifts of LRT riders climbing up and down urine-smelly stairwells. We squeeze our way past cityscapes where buildings—new, old, and just beginning to shoot up—crowd a sooty sky. We leave all that haze that is the mix of industry, humanity, and diesel fuel. We drive the superhighway northbound through the provinces of Luzon, where congestion dissipates slowly. Our shoulders relax, our breathing slows, and we can see the faces of the people on the street. The sky is blue. We roll the windows down and wind sails right through, slapping loose strands of hair about our faces, snatching words from our mouths and hurling them down paved roadways. Handmade houses—nipa huts with thatched roofs and ladders bound with hemp—dot the horizon. Between houses there are rice fields soaking, an expansive volcano sleeping, a river with green kang-kong leaves floating in still waters. Roadside stands burst with bushels of jackfruit, mango, santol, and bunches of red lychee. We can see the horizon stretching before us. And I am breathing.

We travel to Abra, to the farthest northern tip of Luzon Island. Lola Narcisa Claveria sits in the back seat, gazing at the land with a smile reaching all the way across her face. She and her husband left their province years ago. They left their families, their Ilocano culture, they left their land. They started new in Manila.

It takes us twelve long hours to lose the city. To drive away from all that smog and noise, to see watery green rice fields and the occasional pull of a carabao-driven plow and its owner's wide-brimmed hat. We travel so far north there are no inns or hotels or bed-and-breakfast cottages. Lola Narcisa will stay with her family, and I have booked a room at the local rectory. I am staying with provincial priests.

The air is cool and clouds move about lithe as wind. We stop the car twice, once to survey the lush mountains and then to stand beneath a giant black statue of Gabriela Silang charging into battle against the Spanish conquistadors. During the Filipino revolt from Spain in 1763, Gabriela Silang led insurgents for four months after her husband was killed before she herself was captured and executed by the Spanish. Her horse, rearing back on its hind legs, reaching to the heavens, welcomes our van of travelers into Ilocos Sur. I stare up at her giant black face, at the expression of the eyes open wide and the mouth gaping in a primordial yawp. Her arms lift above her head, caught in mid-swing as she casts a sword toward unseen enemies. She is the heroine of all our Pinay warriors. We know we are only hours away from reaching Abra.

Lola Narcisa and her aunt, Lola Philomena
June 9, 2002

Visit to Lola Philomena, 115 Years Old
Balintog, San Juan, Abra
June 9, 2002

THERE ARE NO other houses. The land is silent save the constant crow of roosters and the cluck of hens wandering about the property. Children in shorts and too-big T-shirts hang from bamboo posts and lie on thatch-covered floors of gazebolike structures. Lola Narcisa disturbs the stillness, calling out to the children in Ilocano. It is as if her voice has blossomed from the inside out and the cadence of words moves to a new rhythm. The ends of her sentences twist and arc up and up into the heavens like questions. The timbre in her voice changes from one that is low and sultry to a high-pitched, singing soprano. We follow voices calling back to her.

When we get to the house, we enter a cavernlike structure, passing through short dark halls. We walk into the room where her 115-year-old auntie, Lola Philomena, is squatting on a blue and brown banig, a decorative hemp mat that covers the floor of the entire room. There is no furniture in the room, just the mat and a window to the open air. Three little girls appear from nowhere and watch through the open window.

Lola Philomena's limbs fold one on top of the other, her right knee popping up near her shoulder and her left leg tucked under her slight bottom. She reminds me of a delicate piece of origami, small enough to fit into my pocket. Her fingers pick at white strands of hair, twirling them tight. A light denim skirt falls from her waist. She pushes the sleeves of a royal blue turtleneck up to reveal her thin white arms. It is her face that I am drawn to, a thousand folds of skin circling upon themselves, with wartlike bumps dotting her complexion. Her eyes have lost all color. She can hear us but cannot see a thing. When she recognizes Lola Narcisa, she smiles and sings back in Ilocano, their voices rising up like hope. Lola Narcisa slips down to the ground and seats herself next to her auntie. Though she herself is seventy-six years old, next to Lola Philomena she is a girl, a dalaga, and she easily assumes her role as the prodigal niece. She unwraps pieces of chocolate and feeds them to the old woman. "She loves candy," she tells me in Tagalog. "I bring her chocolate every time." I stay quiet and videotape the two women as they speak. Lola Philomena's fingers press against

Narcisa's cheekbones, pull at the earlobes, wrap around the skull, and pulling her close to her own face, the old auntie sniffs at her skin and smiles. Lola Narcisa pushes strands of hair from the old woman's face.

I feel my heart stretch. The girls peeking in the window are perfectly framed and are also witness to the scene. They feel it, too.

"She is also a victim of the war," Lola Narcisa says, looking up at me. Turning back, she speaks to the old woman. After a while she talks to me, without looking away from Lola Philomena. "I ask her how old she is and she doesn't remember anymore, but I ask her if she remembers what happened during the war and she says, 'Why, did you forget? How could you forget that?'"

When the Imperial Japanese Army stormed the village of San Juan they took every single woman and girl and brought them to the city hall. The only ones to escape were fishing or working the fields. But every single female was captured and made to serve in the Japanese rape camps.

LATER THAT AFTERNOON, Lola Narcisa takes me to the property where her father's house used to stand. "This is a new house," she tells me. "Our house was big, really big, but they burned it down." The old house was made of narra wood, of big thick beams, dark and sturdy, wide enough to hold a household of ten easily. When Lola Narcisa and her sister crawled back to this land shortly after the war, all they found were posts sticking up from the foundation where walls once stood.

I look across the yard at the chickens pecking at the dirt, at the thatch-roofed ceiling above us, and the woven floor beneath us. I close my eyes and breathe. The air calms me. A soft breeze circles our bodies and despite the story, all I can imagine here is peace.

When my father came back alone, the soldiers grew impatient and accused him of hiding the insurgents.

"Please don't blame me," my father told them. "Our houses are spread too far apart—it's hard to keep watch over everyone. Besides, I don't think they'd hide from you. Maybe they're just scared."

Then they asked him how many children he had. And he told them, "Eight."

"Bring them out," ordered the soldiers.

My father called to us, and one by one we came out of hiding and lined up before the soldiers. The Japanese counted each head. Seven. They counted again. Seven.

"You told us eight," the commander said.

"Ah yes, I have eight children, but only seven are here. The eighth one, Estela, is in Manila. I forgot."

"Why, did you tell us eight when there are only seven?"

"I'm sorry," my father said, "I forgot about Estela."

"You lied," they charged. "You lied about that other one, too. Maybe you hid them because they are guerrillas."

Sometimes, when I think of that time, Evelina, I hear all my family screaming at once. The Japanese soldiers questioned my father over and over.

"Tell us where the other man is," they said.

"I told you," my father said. "I'm not capable of hiding people and people who are bad—I don't help."

"Tell the truth," they shouted, drawing knives against his throat. They roped his hands together and tied him to a post. [*Lola Narcisa is crying now. Tears running fast down her face as she speaks.*] "Are you hiding them? Are they guerrillas?"

"No, sir," he cried, "No, sir!"

The soldiers cinched the cord around his body. We children screamed.

"Tell the truth!"

"We've done nothing to you and even if you kill me, I won't be able to give you this guerrilla."

We walk about the property, strolling under large trees, and climbing up bamboo-pole ladders. We cross our legs on the cogon woven flooring. Lola Narcisa pulls out a large cigar and rolls it in her fingers. She places the corner of the cigar in her mouth and lights it. "This is all new," she tells me. "After the war. Because you see, they burned the house down, they burned our family to the ground."

I close my eyes and I breathe. I cannot imagine it.

"The house was over there?" I point to where the new home stands with its concrete floors and heavy wooden doors.

Lola Narcisa nods. "This is where the house was before."

The soldiers took my two older brothers away and left only my mother and brothers and sisters in the house. Then slowly, the Japanese began to skin our father's neck right before our eyes. I pleaded for them to stop, but instead the soldier only continued to peel the skin, slicing him from his neck to his genitalia.

"Children, help me!" my father begged. "Oh my wife, help me!" But there was nothing we could do. I closed my eyes. I tried to think of what to do, how could we help our father? "Have mercy on our parents," I cried. I could hear my mother screaming from the second floor of the house, calling to us. "Have mercy on my parents."

We ran upstairs and found our mother naked and lying under a Japanese solider named Suga, his long flat face slobbered over our beautiful mestiza mother.

"Children, help me!"

The two youngest, Clemente and Esmeralda, grabbed objects from the room and began striking at the Japanese. "Why are you doing this to our parents," they cried. My brother and sister hit the Japanese over and over and didn't stop when soldiers grabbed them by the neck and took them to the yard. The soldiers threw them each into the air and skewered them with their long bayonets. [*Lola Narcisa lifts the hem of her skirt, dabbing her eyes dry, but the tears continue.*]

My older sisters, Emeteria and Esmena, and I rushed back to our father who was still calling out. I fought so hard, resisting the soldiers as they grabbed me; I didn't care that someone had picked me up and tossed me to the other side of the room. One of the interpreters took pity on me and told me not to resist. "Then they won't hurt you so bad," he said.

Next the soldiers dragged my sisters and me out of the house, even as our father and mother continued to scream. "My chidren, help me!" my father cried. "My children, help me!" I heard them calling to me with every step I took. "My children! My children!" Three kilometers away and I could still hear my father's pleas. "I'm really suffering," he cried. At one point, I climbed a small hill with a broken arm. I watched smoke rising from our village.

No matter how many times I hear Lola Narcisa speak, she moves me. Tears run down her face, and mine. She wipes her eyes, talking through all of it. Fifty years later and the Imperial Japanese Army are still raiding her family's home, burning down the house, raping everyone in sight. Fifty years later and her brother, her sister, and her mother and father are dying all over again. "Sana you put this in your head," she says pointing to her temple. "It never goes away."

How am I going to do this research if I cry at every turn? But how will I do the lolas—my lolas—justice if I don't?

Municipal Building
Balintog, San Juan, Abra
June 9, 2002

A FEW KILOMETERS from the house, we walk up a wooded path to the town municipal building. Lola Narcisa tells me that for a long time, she and her husband kept her past a secret. They had six children together. "We were able to raise them well and put them through school," she says, "Tatang was quite industrious."

We climb a trail passing tall bamboo and lush green fronds. We listen to the breeze as we walk.

The Japanese soldiers dragged me and my two sisters, Emeteria and Esmena, to the local municipal building. This is where women from all over the province were incarcerated. They threw Emeteria and Esmena into city hall but kept me in a house across the road in the infirmary. They put people with malaria in that house. Their bodies were covered with large lice. There was no soap. And the air stunk of sweat and fever. There, a Filipino doctor burned tuba leaves and placed the herbs on my swollen arm and dislocated shoulder. He wrapped the broken limb together with dirty rags. For two weeks I stayed in that infirmary. I fought infection. A doctor guarded the door.

When my arm and shoulder healed, the doctor commanded me to bathe. "You stink," he told me, "smell foul." Since I only had the clothing I was wearing, the soldiers gave me a uniform and a pair of shorts. "Bathe," they ordered. And when I was clean, they raped me.

Afterward, the soldiers locked me upstairs with the rest of the girls and women. The room contained many women and girls gathered from all the barrios and towns in Abra. They squatted on the floors. There was no room so they lay down on top of each other. You could not stretch your body. You had to touch another person to fit into the space. And you were not allowed to speak to one another. But in the room, the moaning was constant. There were several other rooms on the top floor and they, too, were filled with girls and women. At night, I could hear the crying, the whole building resisting, aching, crying. They treated us like dogs. It was a room like this, but bigger.

We stand in the open hall, the sun streaming in from a concrete balcony, the sound of trees moving with the breeze. The original city hall, like so many of the houses in the area, had been burned to the ground. This one was rebuilt in the same exact spot as the one that held Lola Narcisa and her sisters and aunties prisoner. "The building was just like this, but this room is bigger," she tells me, "And they kept Emeteria in that room, behind closed doors with other girls." By then her sister had lost her sanity. She was fifteen, three years older than Narcisa, strong and resistant, stubborn. She would say no to them, she would fight them off, and every time she fought, they burned her with a cigarette or branded her with the end of a hot boiled sweet potato. "We weren't allowed to talk," Lola Narcisa tells me. "I'd see her across the room, but she was already crazy. And Esmena, the beautiful sister, was always with the Japanese and I never saw her again."

I stretch my arm out to the empty room and imagine the women strewn across the floor, barefoot, in dusters ripe with sweat and semen. I can almost smell the bodies of unwashed women. "So all of you slept here, like this?" She nods. "But where would they take you when they raped you?"

Lola Narcisa points to the same spot. "They don't take you anywhere. They just do it right here for everyone to see. You lie there and next to you a girl is being raped. I tell you, they treated us like dogs."

Cicadas are chirping. I hear birds fluttering about in the trees outside. "Lola Philomena was here, too?"

"Yes."

"And you were only twelve?"

"I didn't have my period yet. But once they started raping me, I began to menstruate. Imagine," she says. "I would be so swollen. I wouldn't be able to walk. Ganito ako." She hobbles about with her legs apart.

I hold my breath. "So they would take you at night?"

"Or even in daylight. It didn't matter. They were pigs."

During the day they were made to cook and clean and iron for the soldiers. They were made to wait on them. Once, a girl was able to escape through the bamboo-slatted gates. This only made things worse for the captive women and girls. The Japanese became stricter. They got meaner. Narcisa and her companions were never left alone. Because the land was not good for farming, the women grew hungry and began to starve. So did the soldiers. And when there were rumors of nearby rice fields, the soldiers would round them all up. "Everyone must go with them," Lola Narcisa says, "This is the only time I was able to talk with my sister and ask her about her burns."

The prisoners would walk with the soldiers in the heat of the day, without covering, without shoes. They would cross rivers and beds of sand. "But the Japanese themselves wouldn't cross the rivers," she says, "They would order the Filipinos to carry them on their backs or they'd ride a horse."

Intense heat and cold water cracked the women's feet, broke the skin right open and made them bleed. Sometimes they were in so much pain, they'd walk on their knees.

"You've seen the carabao footprints," she asks me, "how the river and the rain can fill their steps with water?" I nod and she tells me, "We'd drink that. Even if there was horse manure there, we'd drink it."

We had been imprisoned for two years. I prayed to God to find a way to make it stop. The pain was unbearable. When the bombs fell, I thought it was the end of us. The Japanese soldiers were so distracted, and everyone ran for themselves. That's how we were saved. I had to lead my sister as we ran. When we could not

run any more, we got down on our knees and crawled. When we got back to town, we didn't have a home. There was no food and our bodies were in pain. We found our brothers. They had been hiding in the mountains. They made a hut for us to live in. Our beds were made of banana leaves. Our food was the trunk of the banana tree.

Interview, Claveria Household
Antipolo, Metro Manila
February 22, 2002

How I met Tatang was like this—one day he lost a carabao. That's what he used to till the land. And so he was in search of a new one. He and his father went to town to see my father, but he was already dead. When he arrived to our barrio, he saw us eating from a banana tree trunk. He took pity on us because his two sisters were also taken by the Japanese soldiers and never came back. He fed us. Every time he came to the barrio he checked on us. And when he fell in love with me, he taught me to read and write in English—we only knew Ilocano then, not even Tagalog. We were married in 1952.

"Nawala ako sa sarili ko," she tells me. She went in and out of madness as her experiences of war continued to haunt her. She'd hear her father's voice calling out for help or see her little brother falling on the bayonet. I imagine her wandering about the forests in Abra on her knees, digging at banana leaves, her sister by her side, hiding in the brush.

You know, my memories from that time are sometimes blank, nothing, and then sometimes I see bits and pieces. My older sister, Ate Emeteria, we've been taking care of her. Now she's well, but every time she hears a loud noise, something comes back. She remembers. I don't allow her to go outside anymore. Because she'll hear a noise and look for a cave or a ditch to hide in. One time she was gone for a week. There were many of us looking for her and people were telling us that she was there in Antipolo. I went everywhere. It took me a week to find her.

She was hiding in a cave in the side of a mountain. There was a cave and I tried to call out her name. "Ate!" I cried.

And then she answered. I saw this white thing. I thought it was a cow, but it was her white hair.

I called again, "Ate!"

And she answered, "Hoy!"

"Ate," I said, "what are you doing there? Come out. It's getting dark." I said it in Ilocano.

"Wait," she said, "the Japanese are there and they are after us." She told me to join her.

"No," I told her. "They know this place. Come with me."

That's how I was able to pull her out of the cave. She smelled bad. She had no slippers. And her dress was very dirty. I asked her what happened but she couldn't remember.

That's why I don't allow her to leave the house anymore. I hang blankets over that table over there. She can hide whenever she hears a noise. As long as she can find a place to hide, she's okay. She stays there. She likes when the two of us are under the table, because she's afraid we might get caught.

At first, Tatang says, you don't have to tell them about the brutality and filth we went through, they might think you were a prostitute. So when times were hard and we couldn't pay tuition and our children were embarrassed, I'd tell them, be thankful. You're lucky you go to school. You have parents. I was twelve when my parents were killed. When we got sick, no one asked us what we wanted to eat. No one gave us medicine.

When I saw Lola Rosa on television—Nelia, Lola Rosa, Atanacia Cortez and—what's her name, the one who died in Marikina? I saw them calling out the female victims of World War II. They told them not to be ashamed, to come out, don't hide—that it was time to fight for justice. But it took me a long time to think about it. Now Tatang was saying, if you come out, what will your children think? That you were a prostitute? That we were not able to tell them of the past? So I let it pass. But the feeling inside me, the hurt would come and go. When we're at home, I'm okay, but when I see the mothers with their children. I tell Tatang, "Ping, what if I just come out?" He told me, let's just think about this. I waited a year. I wasn't the only one who was victimized. They also killed my mother and father. Emeteria has gone mad. If it was just me, I might not have had the strength to come out and fight. I really wish we could come to justice after all this. Imagine, there were ten people in the house and we were all affected.

Tatang didn't know that I came out. He didn't want me to. It was a year before he saw me on the television. He told me he wasn't angry, he was just uneasy. My children were angry. But do you know who was the first to sympathize? My grandchild—the one who lives with me. He was the one who talked to the other grandchildren—they understood. But my children were really angry. Not because they thought I was at fault for the past, they were mad because I had kept it from them.

Once, we were rallying on Mendiola Street near Malacañang Palace when one of the old ladies, Lola Maria, told me she felt like peeing.

"Me too," I said.

"Where can we go," she asked me.

"Can we go behind the jeepney?"

"Naku!" she said.

Then someone heard us talking and said there was a restroom in the Bustillos marketplace.

"Come on," Lola Maria said, "Let's go."

Now, when we were near the restroom, we saw a woman selling squash in a stall. She picked up two gourds and showing it to us said, "I even have fresh eggplant and bitter melon. Come."

Yes, yes, we nodded, but we really needed to pee. We were in a hurry and we didn't want to lose our ride back to Lolas' House. When we came out of the stall, the vendor waved at us again. I told Lola Maria the lady's face looked like Estela's but old.

"Let's go," Lola Maria said. "They're going to leave us."

"She looks like one of my sisters," I told her.

We continued walking through the market a moment, and then I went back to the squash stand. My heart beat fast. I could not stop thinking about that face.

"Where are you from?" I asked the woman. I had a strong feeling.

"Iloco."

"Where did you live?"

"In Balintog, San Juan, Abra."

In my heart I knew. "What was your father's name?"

"They called him Quinio, but his real name is Luninio Adriatico."

"Lady," I said, "what was your mother's name?"

"Maria Teridan."

"Naku!" I said. "Are you Ate Estela, are you my Ate Estela?"

"Yes I am," she said.

We hugged each other, we were crying. We were very happy.

When the Japanese soldiers raided their house, interrogating their father in search of the missing child, it was Estela they were looking for. She was the eighth child who had been in Manila at the time of the invasion. And in this way, on a break from her fight for justice Lola Narcisa found her sister, a woman, she'd soon learn, who also had been taken by the Japanese and made to serve in military rape camps.

Nipa Hut
Balintog, San Juan, Abra
June 9, 2002

THE REST OF the afternoon, we crawl onto the platform of bamboo flooring and rest in the shade of its thatched roof. The little girls from Lola Narcisa's clan who have been shadowing us all day long join us along with one of Lola Narcisa's adult nieces. We lie on our sides or on our bellies, legs touching, arms reaching for the sky. We lie on our backs with our arms behind our necks, our legs crossed and kicking. There's a lot of storytelling and giggling and singing. The breeze cools us.

Here, there are no cell phones. And not every house has a landline phone or television. Here, the night falls and everyone gathers in the home and is asleep before the moon is too high in the sky. People grow old here sustaining their bodies on fish and rice and greens from

114

nearby fields and rivers. The girls cannot understand my words. Not my upside-down Tagalog and certainly not my English. But we are still talking, smiling at each other, falling in and out of sleep.

When I ask Lola Narcisa if she misses living here where life is simple and where the countryside is full of kin, sadness comes over her. I can see the darkness move like a cloud covering the bright sun. She doesn't answer me. She does her best to smile, but she doesn't answer.

We leave her there that night to have some private time with her family, and as I am driven to the rectory in Bangued, Abra, we pass green mountains stretching out before us like giant waves in the ocean. We watch the sky and its magnificent colors slip in and out of the dark clouds, until the oranges and reds sink deep into the soil and the mountains turn to stone. Tomorrow we will take her back to Manila. We will enter the city of noise where children bathe in tires on the side of the road and traffic will fill our lungs with diesel and soot and everything synthetic. We will crawl onto the streets in our silver-blue van and wind our way through rivers of pedestrians—rich and old and poor and young—staring at the road before them. We will bring her back to her husband and six children and multitude of grandchildren. Like Gabriela Silang, she will don her armor once more. Grabbing a bullhorn in one hand and a protest sign in another, she will join the other lolas in front of the Japanese embassy or Malacañang Palace or marching down Epifanio de los Santos Avenue, releasing the trauma of war, naming the source of her pain, making her call for justice, and finally, after more than fifty years, she will find her way home.

VIOLETA LANZAROTE

Born August 7, 1925, Batad, Iloilo

Abducted by the Imperial
Japanese Army, October 1942,
Estancia, Iloilo

Filed Postwar Compensation Suit,
September 1993, Tokyo District Court

forget Me Not

Quezon City, Metro Manila
August 1999

I am Violeta Lanzarote. I was born on August 7, 1925, in Batad, Iloilo. When I was small, my mother was a seamstress. My father was a bus conductor of Panay Auto Bus owned by Lopez.

In October of 1944, when I was in high school, my mother told me, "My child, go to town and buy our food and rice." I went out and when I reached the crossing near the store, I met a group of Japanese soldiers. One soldier said to me, "Come with us. No? Come with us." I told them no. But you see, the soldiers told me. "You cook food, just come," they told me. "You'll just cook for us." When I refused to go with them, they tied my hands and held me down. I was afraid because they told me to come with them or die. They brought me to the garrison in Estancia.

After I was gone for a day and a half, my mother searched for me. She went out to the rice field and saw a young man tending to his carabao.

"Did you see a young lady here?" she asked him.

"Yes," he told her. "I saw the soldiers approach her. I saw them take her away."

My family could not come to the garrison because it was dangerous.

When I arrived in the garrison, they pushed me to the cement. They held my head down and they undressed me. I was raped many times. Sometimes two or three would rape me at

the same time. I was hemorrhaging. This was lucky for me. Because when I began bleeding, a doctor they had captured treated
me. He gave me medicine and told me, "Nene, don't cry. There is
medicine for the pain." When the bleeding stopped I lay down.
It was like dying. I stayed there for three months. I was trapped
and could not go anywhere. My life was miserable. I didn't even
have clothes because I wasn't able to bring anything. Sometimes
they gave me a duster—I don't know where they got it. In the
garrison it was just like you think. They did like that to me. You
know—day and night—they did like that to me.

Then the American planes landed. One day when there was
bombing, someone opened the door where I was being held in a
room with two other women. So I escaped. I was only wearing a
kamiseta, but I ran out the door anyway. I did not take the road.
I took a shortcut through the river, passing all the coconut trees
on the way to Batad.

When I arrived home, everyone cried as if I had died. My
father's aunt Lola Colasa Lanoybo said, "How pitiful you look,
child, thin like a tree." And then she told me to rest, to bathe,
and to take vitamins so I would be strong again.

I was so afraid to come out so they hid me under the house
where the Japanese would never see me. And just like I feared,
the soldiers came looking for me! They asked the people they
met if they saw a young lady from the garrison. The people
would not say a word, but they would give the Japanese their
livestock and rice so even though they were silent, the soldiers
let them live. Then one day, they came to my house and talked to
my Lola Colasa.

They said, "Old woman, have you seen a young woman running from the garrison?"

"No, I didn't see a young woman running from the garrison,"
said my grandmother.

So then the soldiers kicked her in the stomach. And one of
them stabbed her in the heart with his bayonet.

At night, if I remember, I cry. My grandchildren ask me why I
cry. I don't tell them anything.

"You must be dreaming, Lola," they say.

Of course, when I remember what happened during the war, I cry. If I think of the two soldiers who raped me—Takashi and Tagimoto—I see their faces. I still remember. Maybe they're old now in Japan. Takashi and Tagimoto had companions. But those two had nameplates. They were official. I could never forget what happened to me. It's still very painful. It's heavy in my heart.

When I decided to do these stories, I wanted to make sure I got them right. I wanted to honor the women's experiences. So I interviewed them as many times as I could. Each year when I came back, I'd ask the living, "Anong nangyari noon sa panahon ng gyera?" And every year, the lolas told me their abduction stories. And if that wasn't enough, I took the written testimonies the plaintiffs gave Japanese investigators and I weighed them against the personal stories they gave me. Some details were lost. Some were enhanced, but in general the lolas were true to their stories. Mostly because the curse is that they cannot forget.

On March 14 and 15, 2002, I had scheduled interviews in Mandaluyong, Metro Manila, with seventy-seven-year-old Lola Violeta Lanzarote. I had heard her story several times before. I had read her testimony in two transcripts. There was a witness who saw her abduction. And yet, on this first day of interviews she had gone into her dreams and turned the story upside down.

In this version, the soldiers met her on the road. "Please cook for us?" they asked. And when she said no, I have to ask my father, they took her home to seek permission. They let her cook each day and return home at night. In this version, she was never raped. She did not bleed. There was no need for medication. Lola Colasa died of a heart attack.

"Is there trauma in your body?" I asked.

"Only when I remember. I have not been able to erase it until now."

"You can erase it?"

She nodded. "But if I remember it, I cannot sleep."

"Before, Lola, when I interviewed you in 1999, your story was different. Look." I showed her a copy of the transcripts.

"That's my sickness. I am always forgetting. I asked the doctor for a prescription, but he told me there's no medication for forgetting."

Magulo na ang isip ni Lola. Lola's thoughts were so confused. And so I continued to show her the transcripts. As she read them the tears began to flow. "No," she insisted. "I was never raped. I never bled." She shut her eyes and her glasses steamed up. "My lola had a weak heart. She died of a heart attack."

I stopped. I pulled the transcripts away. "You know what Lola, may mistake pala." I kissed her on the cheek. "This is not your story," I told her. "Baka I picked up the wrong papers sa opisina. Sorry, La." She nodded to me then and pulled her skirt up to her eyes. Dried her tears. Then I took her picture and wished her well. And driving away, I called Lolas' House and canceled our second day of interviews.

Eight-Limbed Yoga in Manila

ekam—Inhale—Hands float up.
It takes one Manila rush hour and a half to get here.

dve—Exhale—Fold over.
Floors, bleached bamboo. Doors stained like coffee. Block-glass,
  green-blue sea.

trini—Inhale—Look up.
Women here are small like them, but light-skinned Pinay and younger.
I am a redwood in a field of bamboo saplings.

catvari—Exhale—Jump Back.
Traffic is distant and muffled. Rainy season downpour washes
  everything to the sea. I slip away even as city roosters crow.

panca—Inhale.
A mini backbend. Head up, palms flat. Arms straighten. Heart open.
  Like I am trying to squeeze it out of me.

sat—Exhale.
Five breaths here.
One for the lolas,
two for my teachers,
three for my family—all 100-plus of them—
four for the limbs of my body,
five for the heart.

sapta—Inhale—Lift up.
Nothing holds me back. Well, maybe I do.

astau—Exhale.
Head to the knees and the world goes upside down.

nava—Inhale—Rise.
Like the sun floating to the sky.

dasa—Exhale.
Like a maya bird balancing on a mountaintop.
Repeat four times and breathe before moving on.

They Used Us

GINAMIT NILA KAMI.

They used us. Not like a pot to make rice. Not like a hairbrush to smooth their dark locks. Not like a salve to heal a wound.

When the lolas tell their story, they do not say, "They raped us." They say, "Ginamit nila kami." They say, "Ginamit nila ako." *They used me.*

They took their bodies against their will. They used them. They raped them. Sometimes they say, "Binababoy nila kami." *They made pigs of us.*

Sometimes the translation of words does not hold the energy of the action. The sentiment is lost. The translation, lost.

The words cannot stand on their own. They must sit in a nest of context. They must be explained in action. In story. In cultures we enter only through character.

PRESCILA BARTONICO
Navotas, Metro Manila
April 22, 2002

Born January 6, 1926,
Cabagdalan, Burauen, Leyte

Abducted by the Imperial
Japanese Army, 1943,
Tamburaga, Burauen, Leyte

Tango to forget

THE FIRST TIME you caught my eyes, Lola Prescila, was after the meeting on that first day in Navotas in June 1999. After a big spread of pansit, fish soup, rice, and cakes, after the tables had been cleared and the chairs pushed to the side of the room, after the speakers began to pump music loud, clear, and rhythmic, you caught my eye. You and Lola Virgie held each other at arm's length, and you led her around the room, spinning her about, shifting your weight, moving your feet in complicated steps. The two of you were doing the tango.

I would come to think of you this way. From then on, it seemed as though you were always dancing—your hair up in an elegant bun—tight, black, perfectly set. Your body modestly dressed in a polyester pantsuit, never a dress. Your feet in toe-covered sensible shoes. You hardly wore any makeup, though your eyebrows were shaped and colored to match your dark hair. And sometimes you wore a little bit of lipstick. You were fit and you would dance the whole night away. No one would know the sadness inside you, not if they saw you dancing, pulling all the lolas to the floor, and then the girls. That day you spun round and round, leaning and shifting and moving like a trained dancer.

On our first visit, you gave me and the dalagas a lesson I will never forget. You took me in your arms and you did your best to lead me on that concrete dance floor. I towered over you. I was clumsy and big and bearlike next to you. I have never been good at following the lead. Too headstrong, I guess. Too rooted in doing things my way, I guess. But you dragged me around and raised your arm in an attempt to spin me. I ducked. I tripped. We laughed. I was a lost cause.

Weeks later, you'd sit before me and Ana Fe in that little room at Lolas' House and though you were always the bright star spinning on the floor, in front of the camera you were solemn. Your voice, soft and steady, like the pulse of the music you danced to. Your words were plain. Your story so matter of fact.

Lolas' House
July 1999

I am Lola Prescila Bartonico. I was born January 16, 1926, in Burauen, Leyte. We were four children in our family, all girls. I was the youngest. My father worked as a farmer, tilling land.

In 1942, the airplanes came around our place, to Burauen. The airplanes bombed us at the same time that the Japanese soldiers came. That's when we began our evacuation across the Daguitan River—not far from town. The reason we evacuated there is because that land was ours. Now, we didn't leave that land because if we did, we wouldn't have anything to eat. We planted vegetables to make our own soup. And we made an air-raid shelter in case the soldiers came, but in the end we could not stay there long. We moved from one place to another, but within the vicinity of Tamburaga, Burauen.

Then, by 1943, the Japanese soldiers were always patrolling the area. We knew when they were near because when someone saw them, there was a signal. When we'd hear the signal, we'd run and we'd hide in the air-raid shelter.

Sometime in 1943, three Japanese soldiers were killed in Tamburaga and this triggered the ruthlessness of Japanese soldiers called huwes de kutsilyo. They took revenge by shooting and killing every Filipino they saw.

In the late months of that same year—I was seventeen then—the Japanese soldiers came and we were caught. I was with my relatives. They began by taking the men. They tied them up. And when two Japanese saw there were two teenage girls—me and my cousin—that is when the rape began. They raped my cousin. She was really fighting back. She didn't want them to touch her. I watched and I saw that because she resisted, they killed her. Then, there was one Japanese soldier who approached me. He tied me up. And I could see what would happen if you fought back, so I did not move. I just let him do what

128

he wanted to do. He raped me. I was so scared. When they were done, they tied me up and brought me to the town.

And when they brought us to the town of Burauen, I got separated from my parents. I don't know what they did with my parents, but they took me right away to an elementary school they had converted into a garrison. When I got there—it was probably around five in the afternoon—I saw that there were around fifteen women whom the soldiers raped like me. I tried not to pay attention to them because there were guards all over the grounds. The soldiers brought me to the back of the building, where I was raped again. I thought they were going to kill me because that's where they shot the [Filipino] guerrillas, in back. I thought they were going to kill me. Pero, yun pala, they transferred me to the home economics building. When I got to the home economics building, I said to myself, what is this? It looks closed. Then I saw two other girls there. They were hiding them there. That's where they kept me—there at the home economics building. And when night came, you know, nighttime, there it was again. We were raped night and day even in front of other people. Sometimes, they even brought us to the guard post where they kept their machine guns in trenches made up of sacks filled with soil and placed one on to top of the other.

During the day they forced us to work at the airfield—you know, the landing field. They had us gathering sand and stones, stacking them up into piles. And then at the end of the day, we had to go back to the garrison. And then, they'd do that again. Come to us again. Every night like that. They do like that to us. That was their system. They would rape us. And sometimes when I couldn't take it anymore, I'd forget to eat. And later at night, I'd realize I hadn't eaten. But I was lucky because during the day, at the landing field, there were civilians—related to me, too—who would bring me food.

Then one day, the heat was so bad, I couldn't handle it because it was so hot and I was thirsty. So thirsty. And I asked the Japanese guard if I could have something to drink. Could he bring me water, I asked. The Japanese guard got water, but do you know what he did? Instead of letting me drink it, he threw it in my face and laughed at me.

But what I didn't know is that there was another Japanese soldier watching and he must have felt sorry for me because he said I looked like his sister. Yes. And then he came near me and asked me my name. What is your name? Well, by then I had learned some Japanese so I told him, "O-namae wa Prescila desu." And then he asked me if I wanted to escape. So you don't have such a hard time, he said. He's the one who helped me escape. I learned that his name was Kinipuchi-san.

Tapos he said, later, when afternoon comes and the other workers leave to go home, walk out with them so no one notices you. So that was what I did and when I got to the streets, I ran. I went straight to the municipal building and I looked for my family. I really needed to see my father. I asked my cousin, a collaborator, to help me. He helped me get close to the mayor. He asked the mayor—he asked the mayor—could he get me passes—in case I was caught by the Japanese—because of course, if they captured me again, they would recognize me. Right? I was held captive how many months? They gave me such a hard life.

The mayor gave me a pass—he really was a collaborator, you see. He told me that if I wanted a pass and to have my freedom, I should serve the government—because he was loved by the town—because he was the mayor. "You lead the exercises in the morning," he said. Because the way of the Japanese is before they go to work, they exercise first.

"Yes," I said, "yes, I can do that." Every morning, I would call the people and I led the exercises. I counted in Japanese. I said, "Ok, all of you, over here!" I made them move to my count like this, "ICHI! NI! SAN! SHI! ICHI! NI! SAN! SHI!" I talked like that. And then, after exercising, we would bring them to the landing field to patrol.

I found my father and three of my relatives who were made to dig deep pits in the ground. The Japanese planned to shoot them for being guerrillas. My family was digging their own graves! Luckily, I was able to save them with the help from my cousin and the mayor.

I don't know how long, but after a while, I suppose God took pity on us. Because the planes came and we thought, here come the Japanese again, that the planes were Japanese. Yun pala, it was the Americans! And the planes fired, but there were no bullets! They were shooting blank cartridges. They were telling the civilians we could go home. So we ran. But when we ran outside, when we reached the streets, we saw the soldiers, running all over. You'd think the Japanese were going crazy. So I ran. And then I heard a man say, "Hey, hey, come here, come here!" Oh, it was an American! It was the Americans!

And then, they brought us—we were many—they brought us to the evacuation center in Barrio Arado. That's where we waited until things got quiet. They supported us and gave us canned goods, biscuits, lots to eat—because we had such a hard time during the Japanese occupation. We couldn't get food, we were lucky to get cartons of anything. So anyway, the Japanese ran to the mountain. There was fighting. And many Americans died—we saw them coming back to the evacuation center.

And when it was finally quiet, we went back to our town. We went back. By then, we were able to rest for a little while from our hardship during the war. Imagine how many months I was there in that garrison.

And that's why I give thanks to God that I am still alive. I really had a hard time and that is because I didn't want to die.

And now I want a life for my family. I have good children. I don't have any problems with them.

What I would like to say to the Japanese government is that they ought to right the crimes they have committed against us. They should take responsibility for what they did to the victims of World War II. What we need is tunay na katarungan. True justice. They ought to provide us with compensation for all that they did. And they need to put what happened during World War II in books so that the generations to follow will know. So they will not repeat the same mistakes. We don't want them to experience what we experienced during World War II. I feel sorry for the children. Don't go to war anymore. That's what I want. Let's not go to war anymore. That's what I want.

When I transcribe your testimony, I have to listen through headphones. I have to lean into the screen with my eyes closed as if to get closer to you. I have to ignore the music playing from the patio, the whir of the fan blowing in our little room. I have to ignore the cock crowing, swallowing your words. When I listen to you speaking plainly, clearly, I have to stop the tape, rewind and play each phrase again and again, layering the narrative in my mind, playing it over and over.

There is a dull ache in the back of my mind as I work through your words. With each pass, the pain in my mind grows into a migraine, turns into a stomachache, spins into a kind of nausea.

I am aware that you kept this story a secret tucked away in your body's cells for fifty years. That each night since the war, you have not slept a full night. That instead of nightmares you make dreams through paintings you create in the middle of the night, through music that plays in your mind, through dancing in the middle of a concrete floor with women you know and love, with women who are also dancing the stories right out of their bodies.

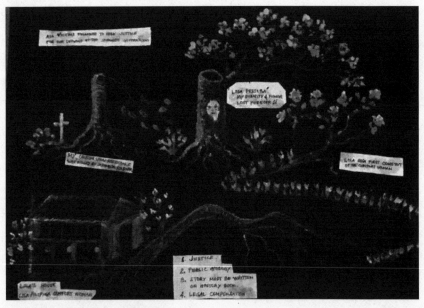

Lola Prescila Bartonico's gift

Drama Day

MY STUDENTS AND I pair up with a survivor, and we take her to a corner of the Lolas' House patio. Each of us sits with our survivor and we listen. They are whispering abduction, hissing aggression, sometimes mouthing words as if speaking might ignite a great fire.

Lola Prescila Bartonico and I face each other like two women having tea. Her eyes tear up, and I gaze upon her, the way her hair has been pulled up and away from her face in an elegant and simple way, the way her eyebrows have been plucked and drawn in thin. I give her my hand and she squeezes it, her eyes going wide. She whispers to me in Tagalog and I cannot hear her so much as I can feel her.

Before she went public with LILA Pilipina, Lola Prescila kept her history a secret from her husband and children. Every night, while the rest of the house slept, she rose and painted beautiful murals, using tissue, cardboard, and children's tempera paints. She created beautiful dreamscapes, images of saints and self-portraits where she was worry-free. She tells me that she didn't want to close her eyes. She didn't want to dream. And even now, with her family knowing about her past, she has not slept through the night. Not since she was kidnapped.

I think about not sleeping soundly for fifty years. How does a body keep that up? Lola Prescila shows no sign of insomnia. During our gatherings she is always the first one up, dancing effortlessly for hours after each meeting.

When our time is over, each of us rises with our lola and we share her story with the group. The dalaga plays the part of the lola as a young woman, walking home from school or cooking rice for the eve-

133

ning meal, washing clothes in a bin or pulling fallen coconuts from the forest floor. And the lolas, the old women rickety with pain and years of labor, take on the role of the Imperial Japanese Army. Then something strange happens. The light shifts, the wind blows hot. The lolas take on a super power and the dalagas grow small and quiet. They are no longer the loud American girls I brought with me. Their chests do not puff out, their voices do not reach across the room loud and articulate. At one point, Lola Benita, as the soldier who captures Ana Fe, lunges at her and the two crash to the ground, taking with them nearby audience members. We have to stop the drama to make sure no one has been hurt.

When it's our turn, I announce that Lola Prescila Bartonico was born on the island of Leyte on January 16, 1926. I tell everyone that the Imperial Japanese Army captured and incarcerated her in the vicinity of Tamburaga, Burauen, in the late months of 1943. Then, the drama begins.

On the patio, Lola Prescila and I pantomime the abduction scene between two Filipina teenage cousins and three Japanese soldiers. I am both the cousin and Prescila at seventeen. First I am hiding in an air-raid shelter, listening to the guns and the bombing. Around me are my extended family, my neighbors, my baranggay captain. Everyone is there. And then Lola Prescila barges in as the Imperial Japanese Army. She is all three of the soldiers. She begins by tying up the men, invisible characters she fashions out of air. She moves to the women, also thin as air, and as she goes to grab them, she suddenly spies me under the table. We are girls. We are small. We are scared and she drags me, the cousin, out into the open and she begins to push me and knock me down onto the cement floor. I shout back. I kick. I scream. I cannot believe the audacity of these foreign men. Lola Prescila, as the Japanese soldiers, fake wrestles me to the ground. I do not give up. I kick in slow motion. I pretend to bite and scratch her face. Lola Prescila holds me down and then comes the part where the soldiers take turns raping me, the cousin. Next to me, I imagine Prescila the seventeen-year-old is crying, though in my suffering I do not notice. And after raping me, the three Japanese soldiers kill me for resisting them.

There is a break in the drama, and I say in English. "Now I am Lola Prescila." I rise again. I am staring at the floor where my imaginary cousin lies with her eyes wide open and her dress torn to shreds. I can

134

feel the heat from her body leaving. I want to touch her, but dare not move. Instead I shake and my skin aches. I close my eyes, hoping the soldiers do not see me. Lola Prescila, the soldier, grabs me and slowly pulls me to the ground. I think about what the soldiers did to Lola Prescila's cousin when she resisted. They killed her. So I let go the fight. I do not move. As I lie on the floor there on the Lolas' House patio, my back to the concrete, my feet planted on the ground, my arms over my head, Lola Prescila climbs over me and straddles my body. She bends over me and I let her hold my shoulders down. She is grunting now, yelling things I do not understand. Her face is very serious and she is not looking at my face, but down, at my belly. She is grunting. I close my eyes so I might disappear, but the grunting is so loud and the bodies so heavy.

AND HERE IS what happens to me, the actor in Lola Prescila's abduction story: I step into her shoes, a little tentative at first. But the story comes out of me faster than I expect, and as I am lying on the cold pavement with the Imperial Japanese Army soldiers holding me down by my wrists, a sharp pain jabs me in the chest. My stomach convulses. My body wants to push them off me, but I know that if I do, I will die. And when I hear the grunting in my ears, the foreign words falling down on me like spit, I cry. I really cry. Something guttural spills from me, an ache that releases and fills the open space. I don't know where it comes from, but I am howling. I forget that she is Lola Prescila. I forget that I am not seventeen. I forget that I am in the middle of Metro Manila, playacting on a concrete floor. I am lying in sadness and there is pain emanating from my body. My imaginary cousin lies next to me and I am mourning her death. The gentle woman that is Lola Prescila looms before me, grunting fiercely, thrusting herself into me and even though I want to fight, I acquiesce, I let go.

DOLORES PASARING MOLINA
Emilio Jacinto Elementary School
May 21, 2002

Born February 25, 1929,
Tondo, Metro Manila

Abducted by the Imperial
Japanese Army, 1943,
Velaszque, Tondo, Metro Manila

The Hunger

On February 25, 1930, I was born Dolores Pasaring, the second
of three children, in Velasquez, Capulong Tondo, near the sea.
My mother worked in a cigarette factory in Binondo and my
father was a laborer on the port of Pier Siete. My older sister,
Narcisa, ten years my senior, sold sweet cakes at the old Mata-
dor in Divisoria. My brother was just a baby.

In 1941, I was alone in the house preparing a meal for the
family when the first bombs fell on Manila Bay. I heard something whirring through the sky. It felt like boulders falling down
around me. The earth shook and the house trembled and when I
looked out toward the port I could see a storm shooting up from
the bay. The ships' pieces shot across the sky. I heard the wind
whistling in all directions, and soon I understood this siren was
a warning to hide from Japanese attacks.

A year later the Japanese invaded the Philippines and my
parents lost their jobs. So what my mother did was she bought
sprouted mongo and made it into ukoy. Do you know ukoy? We
take long sprouted mongo and one piece of shrimp, tapos we
roll it in flour and fry it.

Meanwhile, my father joined other men who had lost their
jobs, diving into Manila Bay to retrieve sacks of rice from ships
that had sunk in the harbor. You know, I could see them all
lined up in the harbor and then the planes came—the Japanese
planes had red circles and the Americans did not—and I saw the
fighting in the air, the fire falling from the sky, but it was hard
to tell who sunk the ships.

I joined my sister selling peachy peachy, cassava cakes, rice
cakes, and tamales, but then the bombs fired down around us

and we had to rush under makeshift tables. I became too scared to continue working the markets. I stayed closer to home, helping my father with the sacks of wet sisid rice. I spread the rancid-smelling grain onto the pavement of the street to dry.

Even if that sisid rice smelled, we ate it. We were always hungry back then. We'd even go through garbage dumps and eat the rotting fruit. That is what we ate during the Japanese time. There was a time we ran out of everything. Even clothes, so I had to wrap myself with a sack.

When I was fourteen, several children and I were spreading rice under the sun when Japanese soldiers approached us.

Before they were kind, but after they lost Bataan to the Americans, the Japanese were cruel . . . they burned our place down. Two soldiers grabbed me and brought me to Emilio Jacinto Elementary School.

At first, I resisted. I struggled with two grown Japanese soldiers. But they only slapped me as they dragged me along the dirt roads. They threw me into a classroom. They hung clothing like curtains to divide seven girls and women. There were three soldiers—an old one, a young man, and the other my mind will not recall.

I wasn't awake with the third one.

Hours later, I woke up and found myself on the tiles of an unwashed bathroom floor, bleeding. Other female victims surrounded me. They soaked old rags in cool water, and they were bathing me. What I remember is the crying. They placed the rag there between my legs to bring the swelling down. Imagine, they just keep coming again and again, just as you are recovering from the previous assault. I think I was there for maybe one month.

When Lola Dolor took me to Emilio Jacinto Elementary School on the second of May in 2002, she pulled me close and whispered, "You know we tried to go in there before, but the guards would not let us pass. Ritchie got mad at them—she said, 'Don't you believe this lola's story? Then why won't you let her in!'"

"So you've never been back?" I asked her.

She shook her head. "Not yet," she answered. Hindi pa.

"Okay, La," I said, "we can tell them I am your granddaughter, and I want to see where you went to school."

"Sige," she said, getting excited. "I'll be the one to say it. You're my balikbayan apo and you want to know all about your family history—where your parents were born, where your grandmother was a girl. I know. Sige na, I'll be the one to say it."

When we got to the gates, she leaned forward past the driver and spoke with great authority. "Will you let us in? I went to school here and I want to show my granddaughter where I grew up." The guard waved us past, and she smiled at me.

At the front entryway, two guards dressed in T-shirts, jeans and tennis shoes sat idly on metal folding chairs. She told the same story and they looked at her and then at me. Lola Dolor didn't even reach my shoulder.

"She's your granddaughter?" asked one of the guards, pointing a billy club my way. He leaned on the back legs of the chair and though he was skinny, his belly stuck up like a little mountain.

"Taga America siya. I'll just show her around."

The guard set down the billy club, moving aside to let us pass. A heavy chain of keys hung from his belt loop. I saw the two exchange a look.

"She's lucky you are still alive to show her around."

Pleased with herself, Lola Dolor said, "Yes, our grandmother wanted to make sure Evelina saw where our lola went to school."

"Your grandmother, Lola? How old are you?"

We stopped walking and looked at each other. "I'm old," she said.

"And how old are you?" they said, looking at me.

"It's not polite to ask a woman her age," Lola Dolor said, "Even if she's just a dalaga, you shouldn't ask." She winked at me.

"And where is Lola?" asked the guard. He was smiling at her now, swinging the stick in his hand.

"In America," Lola Dolor smiled smugly. I prayed she'd stop talking.

"And who is the granddaughter, again?" asked the other guard.

Lola Dolor pointed at me and then at herself. "We are." And then hearing her own words, Lola Dolor stopped for a moment and then smiled.

I looked at the guards, hoping she had charmed them just enough. School was not in session and the halls were barren.

"Okay, Lola," said the guard, "Show us around."

The guards walked down the long wooden corridor with us. We stepped onto the plaza where a bust of Jose Rizal, the national hero, stood firmly in the center of the concrete square.

"They fixed this up," Lola Dolor said. "It used to be all dirt here." She gestured at the ground. "Didn't the Japanese occupy the school during the Second World War?" She looked up at the young guard as if she didn't know.

"This used to be the garrison," said the guard. "This was the Japanese soldiers' camp. Whenever they killed women, they'd bring them to the garden."

I closed my eyes and let the sun hit my skin. I tried my best to sense the dead, to hear the cries of those who had suffered there, but all I heard was the Manila traffic in the distance, horns and tires and heavy belches from their exhaust.

"I heard that they kept girl victims here too. Isn't that right?" Lola Dolor looked at me and winked.

"That's what they say," answered the guard. "Poor girls."

"You see, I told you this was an historic place," Lola Dolor said. Her face grew serious. "I think I heard that, too. Now let me show her my classroom." She grabbed my hand and waved them away. "You can go for a while."

The guards smiled at her then, and saluting, one of the men walked back to his post while the other one stayed behind and followed us from a distance.

"Halika," she whispered. "Come with me."

She took me down the long corridor. Thin glass windows smudged with age and heavy dust muted the colors of the sky and garden outside. From one shattered window, a palm leaf reached inside and brushed at the wall. The ceilings, once ornately carved moldings, now hung precariously above us, threatening to collapse.

I followed with my camera, giving her a moment to walk the halls alone. Her heels clicked on the wood like the pulse of a giant heart beating in the midst of Metro Manila, her gait echoed throughout the chambers and made me think of her, once so alone in a space full of many bodies. She counted the doors of each classroom, trying to open them, but they were locked. She ran her hands along the walls, like she was exploring a cave.

"Ito," she told me reaching a door. "This is where they kept me."

I tried to read her face, but she was calm. There was no door handle, just a hole where the knob used to be, and a metal padlock and chain. We peeked into the hole. It was a schoolroom with a green chalkboard, a world map, and cursive letters lining the walls of the room. "Video it," she told me as I poked the little lens through the opening. The room was big and vacant and the sun streamed through, hitting empty desktops, washing out a world map, just barely reaching a chalk-dusted blackboard.

Then pulling on my arm she told me, "Come, I'll show you." She pointed down the long hall toward a door at the end. "And that is the bathroom where I woke up bleeding."

We crept to the end of the hall and stepped down to a tile-covered bathroom, grimy with film, smelling like sewage pipes. "There," she said, pointing to a corner where a bucket and mop were splayed upon the floor. "I was lying there."

She looked around at a row of bathroom stalls. "Toilets. That is new, but here," she said, pointing to a dirty tiled corner, "it's the same. I woke up there."

I took a breath and saw Dolor as that fourteen-year-old girl, waking on the dirty tiles to feel the warmth of blood running down her legs, to ache from the swelling, to have no sense of what had happened, only that she was hurting. I imagined the women surrounding her, holding her and cleaning her, women who had also suffered the same violation, but were older.

Outside, the sun barreled across the plaza, washing all objects white with heat. Lola Dolor pulled me across the courtyard and her free arm stretched across the grounds. She described how the soldiers would take the girls out of their rooms each morning and line them up to bake under the sun; like grains of sisid rice, they scattered the courtyard, trembling and dirty from the dankness of night. Now there were benches along the plaza, a little stage to host speakers and graduation.

I followed orders, but I was mad. I was angry. You ask any lola, all the difficulties—the frequent bombings, the dead scattered everywhere. And you know, I was always so hungry because there was nothing to eat.

After basking in the sun, they separated us girls from the women and we did our assigned chores. I told them that I had grown up watching my grandfather drying fish and making gluten, and that my mother constantly called me, "Dolor, come clean the fish." So I offered to cook and to feed them and they let me. But at night, I still had to go back into the classroom with the six other girls, and the soldiers would rape us.

Then, one month later, as we were lining up for the usual morning inspection, I saw my childhood friend, Meding. Unlike other Filipinas at the garrison, who were torn and dirty, Meding was dressed nicely as she walked about with a high-ranking Japanese soldier. She did not look my way, not that morning under public eye, but when there was a chance to be alone, she found me.

"What are you doing here?" Meding asked me. "Did they hurt you?"

"Yes," I answered. "You?"

"My husband is an official here," Meding said. And then she added, "Sige, I'll ask my husband to let you go. I can't promise."

Shortly after seeing Meding, I also ran into Ben, a Japanese halo-halo vendor from before the war. I still smile when I think of him. Before the war I used to buy my ice cream from him for three pesos. He was nice. He lived in Herbosa before the war.

He, too, could not believe the state I was in. "I will talk to Meding's husband," he told me. "I will ask him to set you free." But Meding's husband refused to help. They continued to argue for my release. In the end, the Japanese officer gave in, creating a relief pass where I was free to shop the market for the army's meals. "But when you are given an errand," Meding warned me, "you must not escape. Huwag ka tatakas. They know where your family is. They will kill your parents."

During the daylight hours, I went back and forth from the garrison to the markets, focused on the items I was buying, the fish, the rice, the toyo, and the cooking oil, never thinking of wandering away. I knew that if I ran away they could hurt Meding. They could hurt Ben, too—even if he was Japanese. At the compound I cooked rice for the soldiers. I fried dried fish for them. At night, the soldiers still came, and as the war progressed, new girls were brought into the compound, easing my nights. I could hear the girls crying. All the rooms must have been full of victims. But there was nothing we could do. Not even talk with each other, only exchange looks.

She pointed to a corner of the courtyard, an empty space of hot cement. "That is where I used to cook," she tells me. "That was the cantina. And before, we don't have that there. They would order me—put soy sauce there, fry the fish here. Make more rice. They would order me to wash their clothes—but not just me, there were so many of us. We had to follow their orders."

She smiled, seemingly happy to be showing me around. The light shining from behind Lola Dolor washed her out. Her whole body seemed to be lifting up as if from some dark space, but then I asked her, "Lola, how do you feel right now?"

Her voice went soft. I got so close to her, I felt her breathing on me. "My body is shaking," she said. "I'm having a hard time breathing."

One day, Meding approached me in the corner of the courtyard. "It's not looking good," she said to me. "Next time they send you on an errand, don't come back. We are all leaving." She told me not to return to her house but to Ramon Fernandez. Meding had heard my family had evacuated there.

So when I was sent to buy dried fish, I ran away instead! When I reached my aunt's home in Ramon Fernandez, I found my mother in the street.

Naku, Evelina! She did not know me! I approached her. I embraced her. But she barely noticed me. There was a vacant look in her eyes. I held her tight, but my mother's body remained rigid in my arms. "Nay! Nay!" I cried, "It's me, your child!"

"You are nothing," said my mother. "I have lost my child. You are nothing."

My mother was speaking only to the air. She had lost herself to herself! She was starving herself, and this I could not bear.

This is the moment in all the hours of our interview where Lola Dolor's tears run quickly and freely. Her mother never regained her sanity, even after the Americans came and the war was over. They placed her in an institution, and when they'd go to visit her, the old woman would look beyond her husband and children. Now Lola Dolor tells me, "Maybe if the Japanese did not victimize me, my mother would still be alive."

IN THE VAN where Josefa Lopez Villamar and Piedad Nobleza waited for her, Lola Dolor told her friends of our adventure into the school. The three women sat in the back seat and Dolor leaned across to tap them both on their knees as she spoke. "Evelina told the men I am her lola and she wanted to see where I studied."

Lola Josefa's face shrunk into itself and the worry lines carved themselves in rows, delicate and deep. She crossed her arms and not looking at Lola Dolor, she said, "You got in today because there were no classes. Last time you tried there was school."

Lola Piedad sat nearest to the window, watching the traffic as the van maneuvered its way through the streets.

"When we were already there, I asked them if that was a garrison before. They told us, 'Yes, there are actually bones there from the Filipinos that were killed and buried there.' I asked them if there were a lot of women brought there. They said yes, but she already knows the truth, di ba, Evelina?"

"Opo, Lola," I answered.

"She interviewed me so that she'll know the truth. Then I interviewed the guy." Lola Dolor reared back laughing, and slapping her knee she said, "Everything I said was right. Right?

"Everything."

"So you believe now."

"Yes, La. Everything."

"Comfort Women" Memorial
Metro Manila
July 12, 2007

FIVE YEARS LATER, we climb aboard the silver van and begin our journey to the World War II Filipina "comfort women" historical marker on Bonifacio Avenue. With us again are Lolas Josefa and Piedad. The driver winds us through Manila traffic, where small white taxis, stretched vans, open-window jeepneys, and tricycles crowd around us.

The women sit silently. When I flip open my video camera to ask them where we're off to, they smile at me, faces blank as summer clouds. The LILA Pilipina organizer tells them, "We're going to the historical marker, lolas. Remember?"

"I've never been there," Lola Dolor says.

"Me either," chime in the other two.

"Yes, you have," says the organizer, "You are forgetting already. You were there in May for the rally."

Lola Dolor takes my hand and places it on her stomach. "Evelina," she whispers, "I'm not long for this world. I have bladder problems, feel it. Death is near." I rest my hand on her and I can feel the small sack of her belly floating there.

"Lola, every time I see you, you tell me death is near."

"That's right," she tells me laughing. "I do, but this time I mean it. When are you going back to America?"

"Soon."

"So we'll be sad again."

My palm goes hot with energy and I can feel her stomach pulsating, pushing at my skin.

"How will you know when I am gone?" she wants to know.

"What, Lola?"

"I want to see the Lord. I am not afraid and sometimes I pray, just take me Lord. But how will I go without saying goodbye to you? How will you know?"

The van pulls into a small parking lot.

The memorial is set in a city park. A trio of white goddesses with voluptuous bodies draped in Greek togas guard a plaque with a long decree that honors Filipina military sexual victims of World War II. The lolas stand behind the memorial while the goddesses tower over them from afar, young and mean and utterly out of place. I snap a series of stills.

"I cannot read it," Lola Dolor says.

"What good is it?" says Lola Josefa. "They didn't even bother to put our names on it. How can that little thing fit all our names?"

Lola Piedad steps up to the placard and, bending over it, she reads the words out loud with crisp clean English diction. As she reads and her stance grows a little taller and her chest a little wider, her voice shakes like it's ready to fall apart.

"It's just a plaque. Who cares?" asks Lola Josefa. "We are dying na."

"The only thing I worry about," says Lola Dolor, "is the children. If there's another war, what will happen? You cannot imagine what it is like to see children so hungry, digging through basura just for a bite to eat. And you don't know it affects not just those children, but all children."

After the visit to the memorial, we stop at Jollibee and we order chicken and rice and orange sodas, we order fish and green vegetables. The lolas pick at their food and they smile an uncomfortable smile.

Lola Dolor looks out at the crowd.

"Eat Lola," I say. "Aren't you hungry?"

"You know, Evelyn. Even if I'm hungry, when you're here I'm too excited to eat. And anyway, now that I'm old, I don't want so much. If God wants me to eat, that is good, but even if He doesn't, I'm happy because it is His will."

Then, leaning over the table, she brushes my arm with her fingers. "Alam ko na," she says. "When you are in the United States and you feel something like this, you will know, Dolor is gone."

And I smile. "No," I say. "When I am in the United States and I am feeling this," and here I rub her skinny arm and laugh. "I will know, Dolor is here."

Lola Piedad, Evelina, Lola Dolor, and Lola Josefa at the "comfort women" memorial in Manila
July 12, 2007

Transcribe This

WHEN I LEAVE Manila in August 2002, I fly straight to Florida and begin a new life at the University of Miami. I rent a roomy apartment in Kendall, a suburb west of Coral Gables. And after I settle in, I spend my weekends transcribing more than forty hours of interview tapes. Maureen Seaton, a poet who worked with me at the School of the Art Institute of Chicago, is also hired that year. When she hears about my project with the lolas and how I have gone to their sites of abduction, she asks me, "Are you suffering any trauma?"

I laugh at her well-meaning white woman question. What trauma? I am the listener, not the one giving testimony. My role is to see the lolas, to hear them, and to write down their stories. What trauma?

In my office I stack the videotapes. I label them and give each cassette a number. I transfer the tapes onto VHS so that I can watch them on my monitor at home, rolling a little bit of video, typing a line, rewinding the tape, grabbing each lola's words as they come out of the speakers. On the screen, I have to fight through the noise of Manila traffic, which seems to come up louder than her voice. I have to decipher her words amid a rooster's crowing. I have to lean in close and read the lines on each lola's face as she turns and twists along with her testimony. Transcribing the stories takes a long time. Then there is the act of translating them.

I watch the tapes and often, before an hour passes, I yawn. Even as I look at the lola as she wipes the tears from her face with the hem of her skirt, my eyelids are too heavy to stay open. I close my eyes. I nap even as she continues to talk. Her stories of abduction filling my

148

tiny office apartment, painting the walls, seeping into my dreams as I sleep.

At the time, I think nothing of it, though writing fiction never puts me to sleep. I can sit in the same outfit and manufacture fiction throughout a weekend, stopping for nothing—not meals, nor bathing, nor answering phone calls. But this process leaves me fatigued. If I had not decided to enlist others to help me transcribe and translate my tapes, I might still be in that tiny office, lying on the carpet, waking periodically to pause, rewind, listen, jot it down, pause, rewind, write it down.

PIEDAD NICASIO NOBLEZA

Born August 2, 1920,
Madalag, Aklan, Panay Island

Abducted by the Imperial
Japanese Army, January 16, 1942,
Aklan Kalibo

Filed Postwar Compensation Suit,
September 1993, Tokyo District Court

piedad Nobleza, super Lola

I GOOGLE IMAGES of surviving Filipina "comfort women," and your face pops up all over cyberspace. You wear a backward baseball cap and a T-shirt and in your small hands you hold a big placard that covers three-quarters of your frame and reads, "Justice for All 'Comfort' Women." I find you posed like this, standing before the Japanese embassy in Metro Manila. I find you marching before Malacañang Palace. I see you standing on the curb down EDSA protesting the president's State of the Nation Address.

Madalag, Aklan
May 22, 2002

Today, we are standing face to face, in the cathedral in Madalag, Aklan—one plane and one long bus ride away from your home in Navotas, Metro Manila. Here we are, on the island of Panay, in a town so small hardly anyone gets international news on television or in newspapers and certainly not by Internet. We are in the countryside. You and I have been friends for years now, and you have told everyone here that I am your grandchild from the United States. You have told them that I am a writer in search of our family history. Your town mates think I have come to see where our people are from. To see the animals indigenous to our homeland. To pull on the leaves of these trees and know my history is rooted here with you. "She is writing our family story," you tell your former neighbors.

Except for two of your nieces who have escorted us into the church we are alone and you are whispering to me, using your eyes and your hands to indicate what happened here so long ago.

I am begging you to tell your story on camera. But you shake your head, no. I say, "But we have traveled so far."

"I told you already," you say.

Yes, you told me already.

Dagat-Dagatan, Metro Manila
April 25, 2002

My father told me not to worry if I didn't get a chance to study. He told me I could choose any course I wanted in college, but then the war started so I never really got a chance. Instead, I got married to a soldier and we had a son. I was nineteen years old.

When my husband went on duty, I went to live with my aunt in our barrio. When the first wave of Japanese soldiers came, we moved up the mountain because we were so scared. They were so mean and brutal. Oh God. When they saw a woman, they raped her and killed her. They made you walk barefoot. It was during the second wave when the Japanese soldiers caught me.

In 1943 I went back to our house in the lower part of the mountain. I was out for a long time because everything was so quiet, so I took my time, observing everything going on around me. I didn't know there were Japanese in our town because we were in the barrio. I just wanted to see our house. When I arrived there, I spent the day removing branches from our guava tree because the vines and leaves were messing up our roof. Afterward I went to the backyard and cut the tall grasses covering our plants. When my back ached, I stood up, and I looked around. There were no people. Everyone had evacuated. I didn't see anyone so I continued to work. I was so focused I didn't hear the Japanese approaching me and when I stood up next, they were at my back.

Two soldiers grabbed me and said, "Don't run!" Of course I wasn't able to move because I was so scared. I couldn't breathe.

I couldn't move because I was afraid of what they might do. It's a good thing I didn't move—they might have shot me. And besides, all I could do was think of my son—what would become of him? I let them do what they wanted in order to save my life.

One of them was tall, and the other one so small. They were cruel and they hurt me. The tall one held me and told me to just go with him. But the other one, the small Japanese soldier, pushed me around. Of course, I was really scared. I couldn't even take a step because I was so scared. The mean soldier kicked my toe. You really can't move if you're too scared. And then that solider injured my toe. I had to walk about fifty kilometers from where they caught me.

The whole time I was thinking about my husband, who was detained in Iloilo, and then I thought of my aunt and my son. I didn't want them to worry about me. They brought me to a church. All the houses in town were closed. The church was so big and if we go there, Evelina, I'll show you. It's still there. There were many women but I didn't know them because they were caught from different parts of the mountain.

During the day, we could not go out. We just sat there. Then at night, two or three Japanese soldiers would rape me over and over again—there in the pews of the church, inside the church. My body hurt. My hips ached. You can just imagine how they raped us without stopping. Sometimes I cry when I remember. I wanted to run. I wanted to escape but there was only one door and the soldiers guarded it all the time. I didn't know what to do. How do you know what to feel when you can't do what you really want to do? But then, I'd think of my son and I would feel so ashamed.

After two weeks, the Japanese soldiers left the garrison. When I woke up, I wondered why everything was so quiet though there were still so many women inside the church. They just left. The door was open and I ran out of the church and went back to my house. When I arrived, my aunt just looked at me and she ignored me. She didn't say a word. I sat in the corner and I cried. I kept crying and crying and even when I stopped, the tears kept falling.

Your friends and family in Madalag think you are a seamstress. But to the rest of the world, you are an aktibista. A Lola. In Manila, you jet around the city with your best friends, Lolas Dolor Molina and Josefa Lopez Villamar, and you fight for justice. You stand in the center of a circle and you sing songs. You march on the streets. You give your testimony to reporters and students alike. You are practically the poster lola for all "comfort women."

But we are here, in this space. You, me, and God. And you whisper to me—we slept there, by the door. We cooked over there. That altar is new. These pews, they took us here.

"Do your grandchildren know?"

"I haven't told them, but they know. People talk."

"Will you tell them?"

"No."

"But you tell me?"

"You have a mission."

"And you tell the whole wide world?"

"Because it is LILA's mission. Young girls need to know what happened."

"So tell me now, Lola. Now that we are here, tell your story."

Your lips go taut. Your face, dark. You look me in the eye. Nothing.

Typhoons Everywhere

I HAD A bad-energy week. Things fell apart. I lost my ATM card to the machine. I locked myself out of Nursia's gate at midnight—my suitcase trailing after me, my bags falling out of place. When the guard finally got there, I yelled at him in Tagalog.

I thought bad things about people. I said them. I held my breath.

My poor auntie has been in the hospital. Tied up with tubes. Sleeping. It was a bad-energy week. I felt like I was going to snap. Even my meditations could not bring me down, focus me. Fix this badness.

And the rain! So many typhoons coming down on Metro Manila, clustering together, coming apart so fast they don't even give them names. In the States we spend so much time waiting for hurricanes to descend, we break them down into genders, alphabetize them, and chart them. We wait for them. But here, these typhoons. So fast, so furious, no time to name them or color them or put them on any tracking map. They are here and now. The streets are flooding up fast. The baha comes to the ankle, to the knee, as high as the waist of a little old lola.

I canceled a trip to visit the lolas because the water was so high, the rain so thick we couldn't see the road before us. Good thing, too, because there were landslides.

On this fourth research trip, I want to support the interviews I have done with the testimonies lolas have given the Japanese courts. When I asked the organizers at LILA, I got a nod. But no papers. When I asked a second time I got a look.

The thing is, every time I return, there's some obstacle. Some rainstorm. Some form of miscommunication. So many other scholars have come to the lolas. So many reporters and students. Some from Japan. Everyone wants to hear their stories. Everyone wants to help. When we first got here in 1999, we were warned. Too many other researchers have broken the lolas' hearts with their good intentions.

But I made a promise. I told them I was good for it. I've been back four summers and I am committed to their story. I am committed to the fight. "Laban! Laban! Laban!" I hear them in my sleep, chanting their fight song, arms raised, voices big as monsoon winds.

The next time I asked, Ritchie said the women of GABRIELA wanted to know, "Who is this Evelina Galang?" They don't trust me. Inside everything feels all twisted up. If I let myself, I could cry, but I don't go there. I fight.

I tell Ritchie that protesting is not only on the streets. Bullhorns and banners are not the only tools of resistance. There are pens and paper. There are keyboards with letters. There are words that can be written down and shared among all kinds of readers who are open to hearing of the lolas. "Tell them," I ask her. "Tell them: I am not going anywhere."

I am waiting for the answer and all the while the rain is coming down. I close my eyes and meditate. I pretend to breathe. I try, but I've been more engaged in glaring at nasty old white men dating young Pinay all over Manila. I've been snapping at my driver, who is a good guy.

At my cousin Ate Menchu's house, the water seeped into their cars and covered the first floor. They moved all the furniture upstairs and turned off the downstairs electricity. They waited the storm out, wading in and out of the house through the first floor, climbing to the top of the landing, and working their way through stacked furniture into three small bedrooms. It's like being in a tree house. This is the way to fight the rising waters. This is the way to resist the storm.

Eventually, Ritchie hands over the lolas' testimonies, scrawled in columns of kanji and kana characters, translated into typewritten English, submitted to the Tokyo District Courts. I breathe again. I slip into the weekend rain and swim like a fish, quick and light and deep into the big blue sea.

JOSEFA LOPEZ VILLAMAR

Born June 19, 1919,
Cabanatuan, Nueva Ecija

Abducted by the Imperial
Japanese Army, 1944,
Intramuros Manila

Village of Love

LOLA JOSEFA LOPEZ Villamar stretches her brown palm out to me. The hand is wrinkled with lines shooting in all directions, intersecting and spinning a life of almost ninety years. Bulbous joints protrude from each finger, long, bony, moving fast, and with them, her story unraveling in a breath.

"You see, I have two husbands," she tells me. She looks up from her hand to see if I am paying attention, and I am drawn to her eyes, black gone violet with age. "Right here, it says two husbands."

"Where are they?" I ask, smiling.

"Dead, gone. Wala na." She shakes her head as if to call them lazy.

She grabs my left hand and examines it. She flips my palm open and she reads the lines. "Only one husband. I have two."

The van slows and Lola Dolor Molina leans over the back seat to tell us, "Ito na, we're here."

Lola Josefa takes my hand and shows Lolas Dolor and Piedad, "Look," she tells them. "Isa lang. One husband. Ako, I have two."

"What good is it to have two husbands if they have died?" I ask. "You didn't even love the first one."

We have come to the tourist side of Intramuros where the streets are still cobblestone and the buildings resemble a village in Spain. The van cruises by an old museum and café. "Let's go to Lola Josefa's street," I tell Bong, the driver, and he moves back into traffic.

"Anong address?" Bong asks.

"49 Magallanes," Lola tells him.

When we get to Magallanes the three old ladies climb out of the side of the van as I stand there, helping each one step down. The ladies barely reach five feet tall and their bodies have grown small and thin as ghosts. Lola Josefa continues to talk as if our conversation has never stopped. She speaks of her youth back in Cabanatuan, how back then she was curvy. She danced in the zarzuela and people thought she was something of a star. "I was beautiful then," she says. "I was fat, not like now."

Now she is a little bag of bones draped in skin crumpled as newly dried linen. Now her hair is cut short like a boy's, tucked behind her ears and her cheekbones cut sharp angles on her broad face. Now her hips stick out from underneath a cotton skirt and her arms and legs jut out like toothpicks. But now, she is more beautiful because a light shimmers from inside her.

Born on June 19, 1919, Josefa Lopez Villamar grew up in Cabanatuan, Nueva Ecija. She liked to read and thought she might continue her education, but soon after she turned fourteen, her father sent her off to this walled city to work. Her father refused her plea to go to school because education was for boys like her younger brother Cecil. Instead, she moved to Intramuros to live with her married sister on a street of tailors, stitching fabrics and hemming pants, making clothing for other people. Every day they'd take their lunch and then slip off to their apartments for siesta.

That was how she came to meet her first husband. In the middle of siesta. When she was sixteen and napping, she woke to see a man from the shop hovering over her. He was eleven years her senior, an ugly, forward little man; and when she woke he was grabbing at her, peeling her clothes off, raping her. Lola Josefa scrunched up her face every time she thought of him. Ugly man. Her father made her marry him. Ugly man.

The couple had a second-story apartment here on Magallanes and there she bore him three children. When the war broke out, he took the children to the province for safety while she stayed in the city and sewed. After the Americans declared Intramuros an open city, she began trading her work as a seamstress for bags of rice, and each week she'd climb aboard a train headed to the country with other women, also bearing sacks of rice. "Because it was wartime, we'd get to the stop but we would not get out," she tells me. "Too dangerous." She'd toss the bag out the window and her husband along with many others, would retrieve the rice and bring it home for the children. "We were all doing that," she says. "Then we go back."

THIS NEIGHBORHOOD LOOKS no different than any other modern-day street in Manila. Concrete buildings shoulder up against each other. The grimy block with its faint smell of urine and rotting vegetables does not resemble the old Spanish streets of her memory. Potholes lie like mines along the unevenly paved roads. Motor tricycles park randomly on side streets. Neighbors and children hang out on the corners of nearby sari-sari stores. Nothing is left of the grand walled-in city.

We stroll the streets as Lola Josefa gestures at the air like a city tour guide. "These roads were red stone," she says. She frowns. "Not like this."

Before the war, she tells us, there were Japanese people living among them. She describes a restaurant owner, a halo-halo vendor who married a Filipina. "He used to stand on the corner and watch people go by and we would go inside and buy ice cream—ang sarap! I always wondered what he was looking at and why he was always eating. Where does he get so much food, I thought," and then she points to the sky and tells us that when the war broke out he returned to the streets in a Japanese officer's uniform with stripes. "Yun pala," she says, "he was a spy."

Lola Josefa's friends trail after her, holding hands and strolling quietly behind her while I hold a video camera and record her. I don't want her to think I'm not listening so I keep my eye off the viewfinder and I watch her, pointing the lens in her general direction. Later, I find that I have shot a piece of her ear, or an extreme close-up of the corner of her eye. Her mouth slips in and out of view and the words fall from her like rain, spilling fast and steady and soft. We look up at the numbers of the houses and we begin our search for number 49.

"I saw that picture of your boyfriend," she tells me. "The one in the book. He's handsome. What was wrong with him?" she wants to know.

Every year I return to Manila without a husband, which upsets Lola Josefa. "Yes," I agree. "He's handsome."

"Why then?"

"Lola," I say, laughing, "our life was always about him. Siya lang, siya lang, siya lang!"

She lets a yelp escape. Her whole face collapses into worry lines. "Palayasin mo siya!" Her long arms wave him away.

"I have already, La. Don't worry. Wala na."

She looks up at the numbers again, counting them down, finding them stuck to the doorways and the sides of the house and along the gates of tall walls. The numbers are all there, except for when we get to 49. There is no 49. That number has disappeared. That house is gone. She shoots ahead of us, darting back and forth along the block. Stretching her arms across the roads she says, "It should be here: 49 Magallanes."

Lola Josefa scowls and folds up those wrinkles into fine rows above the eyebrows, around the mouth, etching the temples like a cluster of parentheses. Her face gets even smaller. She throws the world a dirty look. Where is the house?

"We were here once before," Lola Dolor calls out, "Remember? We came here before. The house is gone na."

Lola Josefa shoos her away.

"If that is Santa Rosa College," she says pointing two arms out at the concrete gate, "then the house should be there." She looks to the other side of the road. "Because they took me from there and dragged me to Santa Rosa College."

She shakes her head as if the world has done something wrong once again. "Sana nandito na."

Lola Josefa breaks away and walks to the nearest sari-sari store to ask the vendor. "It should be right over there," she says.

Her arms flail over her head, and as I watch, I realize how much weight she has lost since the last time I've seen her. Each year she disappears a little more, growing so slight a gust of wind could push through the city and take her with it. Her limbs spread like a tree's autumn branches: barren, dark, crooked. "I lived there," she tells the vendor, who nods and asks Lola Josefa, "During the war?"

"Before the war. And also during the war. Before with my husband and children. Then after the war started, I sent them to the province na." She leans on the counter and speaks to the vendor like they're old friends. "The streets were clean. Not like this."

Another customer comes up to the window and interrupts her story and Lola Dolor chimes, "Don't you remember, Epang, we didn't find it last time either."

Lola Piedad nods, "Oo nga," she agrees. "Then we went to Dolor's school, right?"

Lola Josefa ignores her friends and continues down the road. Then she stands in the center of an intersection, turning slowly, looking east, north, west, and south. Her arms rise above her head like two long arrows, searching. She talks to the air, points at the houses and counts the numbers out loud. Where is 49 Magallanes?

She waves at me again. During my last visit, she healed my stomachache with those hands. "I don't know," she told us in an interview. "I just can feel it, so I put my hands there and then the sickness is gone. I've always been like that." The hands felt warm on my belly and my insides churned under her touch and what was painful and noisy calmed down. I wish that I could join her in the middle of the street and place the palm of my hands on her eyes, and on her belly and on her heart. I wish there were a way to calm her, to give her rest.

She turns her back on us. She takes a step and freezes as if catching the number 49 rising in the sky. And looking over her shoulder, she tells me to follow.

A tricycle driver has parked his bike in an alley and is dozing under the umbrella of the passenger's side. "Do you know 49 Magallanes?" she asks him, running her arms up and down the road like a flight attendant.

The tricycle driver thinks about it, shakes his head, and shifts in the tricycle's sidecar.

So Lola Josefa continues, as if her story will jog his memory. "At first, they evacuated us to Angono, but when the Americans declared open city we came back here. The Americans pulled out and the Japanese were supposed to stay out, too. But you know, they're pigs. Open city or not. For weeks we can hear the planes coming, the bombs dropping from far away."

She waits. When he doesn't respond she tells him, "All night long you can hear them coming." She hums long and low. "Louder and louder but you never know when they are going to get here." And here she makes her arms into wings and spreads them wide and in our minds the sound of the bombers grows louder.

Now we are all surrounding her and others begin to poke their heads into our little circle to see what is happening. "Natakot ako!"

"Why were you scared?" someone asks her.

The tricycle driver shakes his head. "Forty-nine Magallanes—it's not over there?"

Lola Josefa turns away from him and approaches a lady walking her way. The woman opens a new pack of Marlboros and pulls a slender stick out of the box.

"It's all different now," says the woman who is young enough to be her daughter. "These buildings are all new. Iba na."

"You should have seen the houses back then! Beautiful. Spanish. With big windows. Ang ganda!" She places a hand on the woman's arm and tells her, "One day I came down the stairs and everything was on fire! The whole city was burning!" Her hands swirl in the air as if they are flames licking at buildings, or smoke billowing into the sky. "And it was scary you know because everywhere you could hear this sound, but you can't see where it is coming from."

"Where was your husband, didn't he take care of you?"

"Sa probinsya, with the children. It was too dangerous for them to stay with me." And then she squints as if she's tasted something bitter. "He was no good anyway."

I once asked her if she loved him. "No," she told me. "I was just married to him, that's all."

She worked so hard and every time she brought a paycheck home, he took it all from her, left her with nothing.

"I stole from his wallet once," she confided in me.

"You did?"

"What was I supposed to do? Another baby was on the way and we weren't ready, nothing for the baby. So I took it and when he asked me about it I told him, I took it for the baby."

"What did he say then?"

"Nothing. What could he say?" She shook her head like he was water in her ear and he was clogging it.

And did living with him soften her heart? I wanted to know. Did he grow on her? She made another face. "I was just married to him. That was my duty." She bore him five children before she left him. She told me that when she was in labor, he'd take her to the hospital, drop her off, and leave. And afterward, she bundled up the child and walked the baby home. When his abuse was too much for her to bear, she left him.

"You left the children, too?"

"Why not? They were his children. But I would go to the house and feed them and take care of them. I still loved them. I just didn't sleep there." I studied her face, the dark circles that hung from her eyes, the fine groves in her skin and she told me. "I love my children. They were the only reason to live."

"But not the husband?"

"No, not him."

THE LADY WITH the Marlboros strikes a match, blows into the palm of her hand, sends smoke trailing into the sky. "What did you do," she wants to know, "after you came out of the house?"

"And then two Japanese pulled me by my hair, like this." And she yanks at the small patch of her hair on her head. "But my hair was long and thick then, and I was much fatter and prettier then. And they dragged me through the streets and brought me over there." She points at Santa Rosa College.

"How long did they keep you there?" I ask her and she turns to the camera as if she's forgotten I am there. I repeat the question.

"Not long—four Japanese raped me there and brought more girls— then they dragged me all the way to San Augustin Church. That's how I got these scars." She lifts up her skirt and reveals dark gashes on her leg and scars on her elbow.

"Baboy sila."

"Yes, Lola," I answer, "they are pigs."

KWENTO-KWENTO. STRETCHING memory left and right, turning it inside out, shaking it, repeating it, giving it away. "So it will never happen again," she tells me. The world needs to know.

We look for 49 Magallanes and Lola Josefa enlists every passerby we meet. Each one stops to listen, to nod a head or gesture at the sky. Some wipe a tear away. Lola Josefa bears eleven children in all—five with the first husband and six with the second, and every single child has asked her to move in with them. "What for?" she groused. "So I can sit in front of the television all day long, waiting like a señora? What for? Malungkot yun. This way I can walk out of my house and talk to my neighbors, make kwento-kwento."

This is her freedom. She and her two best friends still take public transportation well into their nineties, maneuvering their way around Manila traffic, climbing onto jeepneys and motor tricycles like girls out on the town. She insists on living on her own, opting to cook her own meals, eat when she wants to, what she wants to. Once she told me, "And when you stay with them, they want to bathe you. Can you imagine? I can wash my own self—nakakahiya naman." She shook her head in great disgust. "No, that is no life."

Though she walks away from every person we talk to, their shadows follow us across the streets of the walled-in city and we grow from a small cluster of four to a community. I feel the spirit of the others with us, of all the neighbors we have met, of the tricycle drivers and the vendors and the children walking to school. By the time we come upon San Augustin's plaza, a whole city block has joined us.

SMALL LIKE AN ant scrounging for crumbs, she paces in circles on the plaza of San Augustin's church, still talking as I lower the camcorder and begin shooting still portraits of her. The cathedral, with its yellow walls and white arches, looms large behind her. "This is where they took the women," she tells me. This is where they kept them, in the church, locked inside with statues of Mother Mary and Saint Joseph and with our Lord Jesus Christ. They took the priests to Fort Santiago with the rest of the men, but the women they brought here, she's saying, spinning on her heel and pointing behind her. I ask her to come forward so we might see her face in the frame, so that we can also see the expansive church behind her. I ask her to step closer, away from the wind, so I might better hear her.

"Back then," she says, "it was the only church. Now there are churches everywhere, but during the war it was the only one."

She guides us through the plaza, stepping around black pigeons scattered on the concrete, moving past vendors who sell trinkets of saints and different versions of Mama Mary, of rosaries and scapulars meant for taking holiness with you wherever you go. We walk around the street children and their garlands of delicate white sampaguita flowers. Lola Josefa places a hand on their heads, balancing her way through them, blessing them.

166

"Inside here," she tells me, turning back to see if we are coming.

The church's interior is expansive, the golden beams and tall windows painted in brilliant colors. Little birds fly about in the rafters, nesting and cooing in the cathedral dome. The sun explodes through stained glass and warms the marble floors. Tourists mill about, wandering up to life-size statues of the Holy family while workers decorate the pews with ribbons and flowers for an upcoming wedding. We stand in a back vestibule and I hold my video camera to my eye. I zoom in on Lola Josefa's earlobe, on a gold hoop earring hanging like a Christmas ornament, and I focus the lens.

This is the only jewelry I remember her ever wearing. She likes earrings. Simple little bits of gold or silver or ruby kiss her lobes, hint at something elegant and understated. She never wears makeup and she's always had that short boy's haircut. She doesn't bother with perfume, but earrings—those she liked. For years she would dress in plain skirts, blouses, and her shiny jewels and travel from Navotas to Lolas' House in Quezon City. Almost every time she got there she had a story to tell. She'd walk through the green gates with her big fingers pulling at her earlobes and her mouth wide open and she'd say, "They stole my earrings!"

And Ritchie would say, "Again, Lola?"

I FRAME THE shot and place her on the left side of the lens. Behind her wooden pews stretch across the church and footsteps and hushed whispers echo in the distance. The light shines from her eyes and she smiles at me, all the while rattling off her story. "Sige, La," I tell her smiling back. "Tapos, ano?"

I've known Lola Josefa for almost ten years, and in all that time, I have never met any of her family, something that seems incredible considering it's so large. Only once did I see signs of her granddaughter because I had gone to her home to interview her. The house was made of concrete. It was simple and clean. The walls were concrete blocks, the flooring also concrete. Walking through the dark house, she climbed the stairs to show me where the girl slept. On the second floor, nearer to the sky, light streamed through glassless windows. That was where we set up the camera. Afterward she took me back down the ladder and seated me at her kitchen table. Above us hung a single light bulb and the naked wiring that made it hot with electricity.

She placed a dish of fried bangus and rice with fresh tomatoes on the table. "They told me you don't eat meat," she said, serving me the milkfish. "Why don't you eat meat?"

"Because one day I made friends with the little pig in my auntie's backyard and the next day, I heard him crying, 'Ayaw ko! Ayaw ko! Buhay ko! Buhay ko!,' and then that night, there he was on the dinner table." She placed her hand on her mouth and laughed.

"Ikaw naman," she told me. "Pigs cannot talk."

I shrugged and smiled. "I couldn't do it." I told her.

She waved her hand at me and laughed again. "Eat," she told me.

She smiled at me as we ate and told me about Villamar, the second husband.

"Of course no love with my first husband," she said. "But the second one, even though his arm was cut off during the war, he loved me and even more, I loved him back."

"How did he make you love him, La?" I asked.

"If I didn't want to be kissed, he wouldn't kiss me. Unlike that baboy first husband, who would keep kissing me, no matter what mood I was in, no matter if I'd say no. What's more, despite the loss of Villamar's arm, he was industrious and he worked to make our lives better. He bought sacks of cement to mix and lay out on this floor."

I looked down on the smooth floor, at the little bit of light reflected on its surface. The concrete cooled the house.

"And the way he cares for me," she told me as if he were still alive. "He wakes up at three in the morning and makes coffee so that when I wake up to go to the market to buy filling for the bread and milk, it's ready. What I like about him is that we help each other at work."

Though everything around us was dark and only the single bulb hung from the ceiling, her face was full of light and she tossed her head back so that her short hair fell away from her face like a teenage girl's.

"The only thing," she whispered, and laying a hand on my arm she confessed. "He gambles. But if he wins, he keeps one cent and gives me the rest and its all mine, but if he loses, I know it already."

"So you were really partners?" I asked and then her eyes grew sad.

"When I was sick, the first one wouldn't bother, but the second one would always say to me, 'If you're going to die, I want to die with you. I want us to die together.' But I was thinking about my children and I'd pity them if I died."

I ZOOM THE camera out to include the whole church. She is talking about liberation, riding a truck to Mandaluyong, of looking for work as a seamstress so she could send for her family, of finding nothing and building a little shack under the Quezon City Bridge. I interrupt her. I say, "May tanong ako, La. We're here now. How do you feel about God?" She keeps on talking—there was no sewing, no work, so she sold tomatoes in a local market. She kept the whole family living under the bridge for one year. She conceived her fourth child there. I let her talk, this is the story she wants to tell. "But La," I say after a while, "now that we're here, what are you feeling?"

"Of course I was angry then. Binababoy kami dito."

Binababoy kami—*They treated us like pigs.*

"The whole church was full of women and children and they would just take us."

"Where did you sleep?" I ask her.

"Anywhere I could lie down—on the floor, on a bench, next to other girls."

She looks behind her and up above. "It's different now." She continues searching the church with her eyes. "The soldiers would come at any time of the day or night and grab us," she says, "take us outside to use us or sometimes take us to an empty church pew. It didn't matter," she hisses. "Those men were pigs. Baboy sila. They'd do whatever they pleased."

"How did you survive?" I ask her.

"My older sister was here, too. I really thought that we were going to die here, but I prayed to God. I told Him to think of my children. I always prayed."

She tells me her anger saw her through. She was matapang. Strong. Courageous. That's how she survived. And then finally she says, "At sa awa ng Diyos." She points to the ceiling. And I nod, yes, and through the mercy of God.

And then she wags her finger at me and talks about the importance of a good husband. I take a breath and for a moment there is an image of a man with an arm, pouring coffee in a cup, leaning over Lola Josefa, offering her a taza of kape and a kiss on the cheek. "That's why," she tells me. "You have to find the right husband. He has to be good to you and then you will be happy."

"But I am happy," I tell her. "I have many boyfriends."

She makes a face and throws her hands up. I can see the bones on the underside of her wrist. "You only get one husband, you better be careful."

I look at the palm of my hand to see him sitting there, a faint line moving toward my heart line. Was that him? "I only need one, Lola," I tell her. "Besides," I lean in to kiss her cheek, "all you've had is bad luck with men. Why do you want me to marry?"

She laughs and then sighing she looks up at the windows, at the light streaming from them. "One day it was so quiet. Nothing. No noise. No one coming in. I thought, what's wrong." She climbed up on a pew and peeked out the window and saw no one. "Yun pala." The end of the war, MacArthur had landed.

BACK ON THE streets she tosses her arms at the road. "The Japanese had soldiers there before—so how can you run away. Hindi puwede." And to the right is the convent where the nuns were also taken, made bloody from rape, made pregnant from that war.

I try to imagine the guards at the end of the road, their long steel bayonets pointed to the sky, their boots hitting the cobblestone road. I try to imagine the fires lapping at the buildings and the men and women torn apart and separated.

"What do you feel?" I ask her. "Now that we are back."

"I am remembering," she says.

"How do you feel?"

"I am trembling. Sa dibdib. I am shaking. I am remembering."

ONCE I ASKED her if her experiences with her first husband and the Japanese soldiers affected her desire to lie with Villamar. Was that painful, too? She shook her head no. She said it was delicious. "You let him hold you?" I wanted to know and she said of course, he loved her. She loved him. And your first husband? Her light went dark. "I was just married to him. With that one, I was always out of the house, working, sending money to the children. With that one I carried out my duties as wife—all without pleasure—and I bore him five children. But with Villamar, I created six more and that, to me was love."

I wonder how much walking she did when Villamar was with her, if she was on the streets making kwento-kwento with all her neighbors, traversing all over Manila then, too, or if she was content to stay at home. That day in Intramuros, we search all over the walled city for 49 Magallanes and never find it. And that is not the first time she has been back since the war. She's been back several times and each time she looks for the house but cannot find it. World War II burned everything down and almost all the buildings here are new.

WE TRAVELED TO Intramuros in 2001, and in 2007 the three friends —Josefa, Dolor and Piedad and I—board the same old van and drive to the site of the World War II "comfort women" memorial. We stand around the monument and I can tell that while Lola Josefa thinks it's a nice gesture, she doesn't see what it has to do with justice or an apology from the Japanese government. She isn't angry, but indifferent. No, she is more concerned with the palm of my hand, how the lines are mapping out my future, how the husband is on the horizon.

"Only one," she says looking up at me. "I have two. Are you married now?"

"Not yet." And then she stops and searches my face. Looks into my eyes and sees something. She says, "You look so familiar to me—do I know you?" I don't miss a beat, though my heart aches. Smaller and smaller, she is shrinking into herself.

"Yes, you know me. You love me."

"Yes, I know I love you, but tell me again. What is your name?"

Lola Josefa's best friend, Lola Dolor, squeezes my hand, looks at me out of the corner of her eye and says, "Malapit na, si Epang." I nod, yes. Death is near. Freedom is near.

The following summer I will return to Manila for the fourth time in ten years. Lola Josefa will be ninety years old. It will be the only time in all my visits that she will not come to Lolas' House. It will be the only time I will not see her and she will not read my palm. It will be the only time she will leave the hospital and finally join her children in the province.

"Evelina, La. Ako si Evelina," I tell her.

"Oo nga," she says, nodding. "It's you, pala."

I close my eyes and I feel the breeze blowing through the streets of Manila, sweeping her away from us like a beautiful kite, her small figure twirling in the wind, her stories raining down on us from the brilliant blue sky.

Paalam

Macabebe, Pampanga
July 2002

THERE ARE DAYS when I step away from the lolas and I search for my own grandparents. On these days, I am doing my best to stay grounded, to remember that I am a foreigner on these islands. Then again, I am not, considering that World War II did not affect only the lolas, but my lolas and lolo, too, my parents—and through inheritance and attitude, me too. There are days when I need to breathe.

One Sunday, the driver stirs the silver-blue van through the streets of Metro Manila, out onto the superhighway. We are traveling to the province of Pampanga. The rain has been coming down for days and in the city, water has risen knee-high. Debris floats in the middle of the street. When we get to the exit for Macabebe, the van begins the slow winding to my father's boyhood home. Here, the streets are also rivers. The wheels of the van slice through the waters. We pass city hall where a statue of Jose Rizal hovers over floodwaters. The driver makes the sign of the cross as we roll slowly past the church. Water is everywhere. The houses on either side of these unpaved streets float like barges. When we get to the Galang house, I see a plank no wider than a foot placed loosely between the street and the front step. My Uncle Armando sits on the porch in a T-shirt and shorts, his flip-flops dangling from his feet. When he sees the van pull up, he waves and tosses his cigarette off to the side of the house into the muddy waters.

The house looks like a dollhouse, drifting elusively in the water. I balance my way up the single beam. Even in the country, the waters are so dirty. Next to the porch, a little rowboat drifts with the breeze.

Uncle Armando announces my arrival, and I make mano. I go to Lola

172

Charing, my father's auntie, and I raise her hand to my forehead. This is a sign of respect, a way of showing love. A good Filipino child never comes without asking for blessing, never leaves without making paalam. Lola Charing treats me as if we have known each other all our lives, though this is the first time I have seen her since I was three years old. She wraps her thin and wiry arms around my shoulders. She sniffs my skin, suddenly grabs my face with her two hands, and kisses me.

Long suffering from tuberculosis, Lola Charing spends her days on a wicker cot, surrounded by photos of me, my brothers and sister, and my cousins in America. She shuffles through those photos every day like tarot cards, reading the faces of each of us, memorizing each rite of passage we encounter—baptisms, first Holy Communions, graduations, weddings. The stacks of photos pile six inches high.

Behind her cot, watermarks stain a dresser, evidence of all the floods that have entered this house. Lola Charing is my oldest living relative on the Galang side. Today is a good day and she is feeling feisty. She points to the graduation photos of my father and his brothers and sisters. They are lined high up above the doorways. Surely the floods will never reach them.

When I see the photos of my uncles, I am astonished. In their youth, my titos resemble my own brothers—young men in their twenties, dressed in caps and gowns, cast in sepia tone. A photograph of Lola Charing graduating from pharmacy school, long before her bedridden days of tuberculosis looks down on me. Is it possible that I am seeing my own face? The high cheekbones, the angular jaw, the lips. Are those my lips?

"You go visit your lola and lolo na," she tells me, after we talk for a while. "Armando will take you."

THE HOUSE IS across the street from the town's elementary school. My dad and his siblings attended the school. From the porch, I see the wide clay fence that separates the school from the street. There is one gate, the only entrance in and out of the campus. During World War II the Japanese occupied the school. My lolo was the town dentist and town politician. After the war during Philippine Liberation, he joined guerrillas in the mountains, fighting alongside U.S. soldiers. My lola had her own tailoring business and when she wasn't managing her seamstresses, she was selling fish and meat at the market. She was always working and always pregnant. Four out of twelve of my grandparents' children would have been born by World War II. My dad was the oldest. He was mischievous and bold, even then. All my life he has told tales of sneaking off without his parents' permission to fish for supper, bumming cigarettes and chocolate bars from U.S. soldiers, or learning Japanese songs in school. My Auntie Dolly, my father's younger sister, on the other hand, remembers being in their house and looking into the schoolyard. "We saw the Japanese torture their prisoners by making them sit in the hot sun for hours," she tells me. "Then they'd throw big barrels of water on them. We saw that." The prisoners were all men, no women.

Japanese soldiers came to the house and my Lolo had to fix their teeth. That was how he stayed on their good side. "But one time," my aunt tells me, "I remember this Japanese officer came to our house drunk, calling to your lolo. 'Doctoro! Doctoro!' he shouted. He was looking for a woman, you know. The steps to the house were high and many and your lolo told us to go upstairs and hide. And then he went to talk to him and you know your lolo—he was not afraid of anything—he argued with him and sent him away."

What my father doesn't tell me is that every time the planes shot at one another in the sky, the whole family ran to the ditches they had dug in the backyard and hid. "We were so scared!" my aunt says.

"Even my father?"

"Of course," she says. "He was with us, wasn't he?"

I say that—even my father—because he has never told us those stories. Stories of fear and hiding. His tales of war are always romantic, and daring. In them, he is a Filipino Huck Finn.

UNCLE ARMANDO AND I climb into the little rowboat. He paddles us through the streets with ease. We drift down the canals and wind our way into the cemetery. The graves rise high above the ground. He maneuvers the rowboat around concrete caskets. Branches of trees submerged in water hang low and every now and then we must duck. At times, we find ourselves tangled in the brush.

"Nassan sila, Uncle? Malapit na tayo?" I am searching past all the graves, looking for a marker. There are stone angels and Mama Marys

174

standing among the tombs, gazing out onto the water. No sign of the Galangs.

ONE OF MY first memories is of being in Macabebe. My parents and I were visiting. I was just learning to walk. The adults sat along the walls of the room—there were so many of them—uncles and aunts and my lolo and lola. They talked with loud voices and their words had many syllables. They spoke Kapampangan, the dialect of Pampanga. The words sounded different than Tagalog, the language of my mother's family. The cadence of their sentences was fast and confusing. Was nothing like the little bit of English I was being fed. I couldn't understand. There was a single light hanging from the ceiling. There was laughter and all their arms seemed to reach out to me. I remember the laughter. I remember thinking about crying because they startled me so.

In Manila, I was the youngest cousin of dozens of children, but in Macabebe, I was the only one. "Mekeni!" called my Lola Kula. "Mekeni!" said my Lolo Miguel. Come, they called to me, come here. Too small to understand, I went with their laughter, with the lilt of their voices, with their wide smiles and deep dimples. "Mekeni!" they cried. I remember running into their arms.

"ITO NA," UNCLE Armando says, pointing past a tree, shifting the paddle right and left and turning the boat around a large headstone.

They are just around the corner. The grasses are thick. We are stuck. We cannot get to them. But from here I can see my grandparents: Miguel and Nicolasa Galang. They have been laid in one tomb, one long cylinder. Their names are etched where the tomb has been sealed. The weeds are too high and the water so black. We cannot get to them. But I am near and I can feel them. I can almost imagine their ashes swept together, dusting the floor of that tomb.

"Mekeni," I hear them calling. "Mekeni."

"Nandito ako," I tell them in Tagalog. "Nandito ako." I am here. I am here. Floating, but I am here.

Japanese
Leftovers

TIRA NG HAPONES. Not cold soba noodles. Not half-eaten rolls of sushi. Not day-old tempura.

Tira ng Hapones are the women they used. Tira ng Hapones are the women who gave them "comfort." They are the women they captured and placed into garrisons and raped repeatedly.

When the war was over and the doors swung open wide, they were the women who escaped.

The women who were freed.

And when some of the women returned to their homes, the doors shut in their faces. The mothers spoke through cracks in the bamboo, told some of them to go to the city, to live with another family, to carry on without them. Ay, kasi, tira ng Hapones.

And when some of the women walked to the market or to church or to meet their other families, the children on the streets threw rocks at them, whispered stories they had heard. Called them Japanese leftovers.

ATANACIA CORTEZ
Fort Santiago
March 19, 2002

Born August 15, 1923,
Pampanga, Luzon Island

Abducted by Imperial
Japanese Army, 1943, Manila

Filed Postwar Compensation Suit,
April 2, 1993, Tokyo District Court

The Not-so-Glamorous Life of Atanacia Cortez

I AM AT my mother and father's dining room table, logging all the photos and videos from my July 2007 trip to the Philippines. That summer, my cousin Anna Karina shot a series of photographs of me dancing with Lola Ashang. She used natural light and stood a respectful distance from the two of us. Anna Karina held her camera up, pressed the shutter, clicking away to the rhythm of the music. In the still of the frame, Lola Ashang and I are spinning in each other's arms. I tower over her and wrap my limbs around her like long scarves winding about her neck. We must be moving very fast in the low light because Anna Karina's photos are a blur. Our faces streak across the frame, caught in midmotion, soft and grainy and imperfect. I back away to the edge of the dance floor, Lola Ashang shimmies to the opposite side and then holding up her two arms she challenges me. We take giant steps toward one another. In each frame, the bodies are caught in wild expression. I bend my knees a little lower, hunching down and waving a fan at my chest. I stoop lower and lower to meet Lola Ashang's gaze. We end up nose to nose, forehead to forehead, her breathing so close to my skin, until she is sniffing at my cheek and we are caught in an embrace, laughing. You can practically hear the music vibrating in the photos and it is as if joy has taken over the entire room.

In the photos, Lola Atanacia Cortez dances for hours. Even as the others must take a seat and rest, Lola swirls about the floor, jaw jutting out, eyes closed, fists in the air. She spins like a hot tropical typhoon.

Her passion for dancing is almost as strong as her passion for justice. Earlier that day, only months after Prime Minister Shinzō Abe declared there was not enough evidence to prove the women had been coerced into military rape camps, the lolas gathered around a laptop, peering over each other's shoulders, screening news stories about how Abe's statement had set activists around the world on fire. The stories were in English, and while many of them did not speak the language, the lolas nodded their heads, listening to every word, recognizing their own faces on the screen, and reading the visual images like text.

Afterward, they sat in silence, and the words of the Japanese prime minister sank into their bones. "Not enough evidence to prove coercion." A few of the women whispered under their breath, sighed and then without warning Lola Ashang burst like a flame.

Her eyes darted around like she was looking for Abe, and her hands flew up into the air, the fingers spread wide open, twitching like spider legs.

Finally, it's your day and they still kick you down like that? What are you going to do? How are you going to fight that? Sometimes your own husband comes to you, and you don't even want him, how much more strangers like that?

A soft chorus hummed under Lola Ashang's tirade. Her voice spun itself tight and circled the tiny patio, bouncing off the wall and reverberating in the ceiling fans. It was like she was on loudspeaker.

I'll tell you what I don't like [*she opens and shuts her Spanish fan*]. We are so old and they treat us like that? [*She spreads her legs apart and points the fan between them.*] Do they want everyone to think we invited this on ourselves? Are you kidding me? It was war. Do you think we had a chance?

I am Atanacia Cortez. I was born in Santa Rita, Pampanga, on
April 15, 1923. My parents were poor rice farmers and when
I was five years old, my father sent me to work for a rich relative in Angeles, a neighboring town. I was brought there to
be household help. I did simple chores, serving my aunt and
uncle, crawling under the house to retrieve duck eggs. One day
I noticed that there was a school next to us and when my father
came to see me, I asked him why I couldn't attend classes, not
even for a little bit. We were poor farmers: My father insisted
I work. By the time I was ten years old, I returned to help my
mother, laboring in rice fields. And then when my uncle from
the Fernandez family won the lotto, my father sent me back a
second time. By this time, I was already a dalagita, a young lady.

I was washing the dishes in the washbasin one day when my
Uncle Dodong—he had bad intentions for me—suddenly he
embraced me from behind. I was still young of course—I didn't
even have my breasts, you know—I didn't understand what he
was doing.

Tapos, when I ran back to my father and told him what
happened, there was a fight. Then what we had to do, we had to
move out of the house and live down by the pushcarts because
my uncle owned that house.

We were seven in the family, and I was the oldest. We were so
poor, we didn't even have money for—you know bakya? Wooden
sandals. We had nothing for clothing. Soon after I rejoined my
family you know what I did? I took my father's fighting cock and
brought it to the waterfalls in Porac. I plucked its feathers, and
I cooked it.

The cock was a game fighter, a scrawny bird let loose in a ring,
fighting other cocks to the death. It brought a little income to
my family, but so what? We were hungry. And you know how it
tasted? Masarap! [*Lola Ashang licks her lips.*] I cooked it. And my
father got mad at me.

He banished me from the house. I could no longer sleep there. He refused to talk to me. He sent me to my godmother's house. He hung a bolo from the stairs, a sign to everyone that I was not allowed in his house. I was told I could not come home, not as long as the bolo was there. That was how it was during our time. And if the bolo is hanging from the door, nobody can court you. After a week, my mother fetched me. I thought my father would welcome me, but I was mistaken. Now, you know what he did? He closed the door—our door was made of bamboo. And he closed the windows. And he got the broom made of the ribs of palm trees, and he hit my body and made red marks everywhere! That night I escaped when everyone was asleep and ran to my grandmother's house. My mother kept telling me to come home, but my father said stay away.

By the time I was eighteen years old, I was already married five years to Guiller Murillo. After my husband left to join the war in 1941, my mother-in-law and I moved to Santa Potenciano to live with his cousins. For two years, we lived without knowing if he was coming home. In my mind, it didn't matter because I didn't love him anyway.

Then one night in 1943, he showed up at the house long-haired and smelling foul. He said he had been captured by the Japanese and made to march to Bataan, but that he and several of his companions had escaped. All the while he was making his story, I listened, but I felt nothing.

Because, Evelina, when I was thirteen years old, the Murillo brothers who lived right next to the refreshment parlor where I worked teased me every day. I was thirteen and the two of them courted me, but I wanted nothing to do with them. I was too young. Then one night around 2 A.M., I was on my way home from work, dreaming of dresses I would buy with my wages when I noticed a car following me. Two men stepped out of the car and approached me. Tapos, they put a kerchief to my mouth like this and they whisked to Guiller's uncle's house and forced me to marry him against my will.

Now he was telling me he loved me. He wrapped his arms

around me as if to embrace me, but my body resisted the embrace. Instead, I remained stiff.

The following night there was a brownout and the house was dark and silent. I looked over at my husband, at the way Manong Romero, his cousin, had cut his hair earlier that day. Ay, he was handsome after all. He looked like Leopoldo Salcedo. But it was nothing to me. Anyway, in the middle of the night, I heard a noise.

When I looked out of my window, I saw Japanese soldiers climbing out of a truck parked in front of the cousins' apartment. And I saw the lights of another truck coming down the dark road. "Guiller," I whispered, "Guiller, there's many Japanese, they're coming down!"

Suddenly the lights came back on and when I looked down the staircase, I saw a white flag with a big red circle. Several Japanese soldiers charged up the steps and just beyond the soldiers, I could see prisoners being dragged up to our apartment. Later I would come to see that they were my husband's companions, others who had escaped with him from Bataan.

Yun na—I ran to Guiller, who by now had joined me in the sala. We fell into a tight embrace as the Japanese barged into our home. A small Pilipino policeman, dressed in khakis and a baseball cap, accompanied the intruders. Stepping forward, he pointed to my husband and said, "He was one of them." The soldiers pulled my husband from me just as my mother-in-law entered the room.

"What's going on?" she demanded as the soldiers began to tie Guiller up. She took a step toward them and a Japanese soldier shoved her and she fell to the floor near an open window.

"Is it okay if I get dressed first?" asked Guiller. "Sia," he said to me, "get my clothes and my shoes in the bedroom. They're hanging on the back door."

So, I jumped up and answered, "Yes," but I was thinking, what am I going to do, are they going to kill him? I went to our bedroom, looking for I didn't know what. Tapos, when I saw an iron pipe stuck underneath the sink—ito—I grabbed it and hid the pipe behind my back. I went back to the sala. Though he was not yet dressed, the soldiers had tied his hands behind his back, but his feet were still free. "Where's my clothes?"

"I couldn't find them," I lied.

"Never mind," barked the police. "Let's go." And when the policeman leaned down to tie my husband's feet, I took the pipe and whacked him on the head. I surprised myself—naku—at how thick and heavy the pipe was and how easily I lifted it over my head to hit the man. Immediately, the Japanese soldiers seized me, kicking at my breasts and pushing me down.

And then, he fought for me, my husband fought for me! Guiller's hands were still tied behind his back, but he kicked at the soldiers and did his best to push them away.

One of the Japanese drew a bayonet and slashed at Guiller. Blood trickled from one side of his jawbone. "Enough," I yelled. "Stop it!" The soldiers responded to each of my cries with a punch to my chest, "Enough already," I yelled. They hit my stomach. "Stop it!" They punched me in the face. "Kill me now!" I shouted.

My husband's blood continued to splash everywhere, marking everything, and the sight of it made me faint. When I awoke, my body was bruised and aching. My hands were tied behind my back. My feet tied at the ankles. I looked around and found the Japanese had thrown us like two sacks of potatoes into the back of the truck.

We were brought to the Quarter de España in Intramuros where we remained tied up and separated to the corners of the room. There, the Japanese made me kneel on wooden benches covered with coarse grains of salt. In my duster, my bare knees balanced on salt. The grains bore holes through my skin and left little red gashes. Anak, I remember looking up at one point and being pummeled with the barrel of a gun. Soon my mother-in-law entered the quarters with a plateful of food. Neither my husband nor I were allowed to go near her, only to watch her devour the meal on her own.

When the sun was high in the sky, and I was too weak to stand or to speak, they moved us from the quarters and placed us into a large car that took us to Fort Santiago. One by one, we were made to walk our way to the car. My husband traveled separately, but when we reached the garrison, we were reunited. Two soldiers held me up because I was too weak to stand or sit on my own. Others undressed my husband so he stood before them naked except for the rope that tied his feet together. They hung him from the ceiling so his head was low to the ground and then took turns beating his chest with their guns. He swung like an animal in a meat locker and then I saw it, the blood, seeping from his chest, running all over his body. Naku, Evelina, I felt the tears swelling in me, rolling down my face and I began to scream at them, "Stop it, enough, stop it!" Not only did they continue to beat my husband, but every time I said anything at all, they'd hit me! They didn't just slap me, they beat me! I shouted and shouted until they brought my husband down.

And I thought they were finished, but no. They took him to a tree and spread his fingers out like this. [*She stretches her two palms out, fingers grasping at the open air. She is crying as she does so.*]

Naku! They pulled out his nails like this, one by one! In this way, they tortured my husband, they hung him before me like dead meat. They slid each fingernail from his hand and scored a knife down his torso to skin him alive.

I could not bear it. I passed out.

When I woke I found myself locked up in a small stone room. A janitor swept the floors near me and asked me, "Do you want to eat, Ate?" But I refused.

"Where is my mister?"

"Later, Ate. They will walk them through here, you will see."

When the soldiers paraded past, they dragged the bodies of the dead. Guiller was second from the last.

I watched them stuff the bodies into an underground passage. I heard the bodies, falling down a long stone stairwell and falling to the sea.

The Japanese kept us under the stairwell at Fort Santiago, holding us in little stone rooms not fit for caged animals. On the night my husband's body was tossed into the sea, two Japanese soldiers took me from my cell and brought me above. There were two rooms made of sawali, strips of bamboo. I recognized one of the Japanese, a man who took Spanish lessons from my mother-in-law.

He caught me looking at him and said, "What is that? Come, come." Tapos, I followed him to the second door. Once inside, the old man pushed me onto the bed. I could not do anything, Evelina. Even if I was married, you know, I was still young. He crept up to me. Slowly, he undressed me, stripping each piece of clothing from me and dropping them from the edge of the bed. I closed my eyes and waited. There was the sound of nothing. And then he was gone. I thought he had left me, but soon he returned fresh from a bath. He locked the door after him, and all I could think about was escape. But how?

Then he raped me.

He was old, and he was the general at Fort Santiago. I cannot forget him. And when he was done, two more soldiers raped me.

For seven months the Japanese kept me in a room above the dungeon where other prisoners—Filipinos and Americans— were imprisoned. In the same garment, I was raped several times a day. I never bathed, I never washed. My cotton duster grew stiff from all the sweat, the blood, the semen. I stunk, and I wondered how the men could take me like this.

I wanted to bathe. But then I would have to take my clothes off and they would watch me. How can I do that? You take your clothes off, they rape you again.

They took me anyway. And when I resisted under their weight, it seemed to me they liked that even more.

Mostly the soldiers who raped me were Japanese, but some-times they were Korean, too. I did not take my own life, I did not strangle myself. If only I had something to hit them with. I thought about slipping away after they raped me, but at the end, I was always so tired. I couldn't. They gave me food, but I did not eat.

UP CLOSE, YOU can see the roadmap of her face—a thousand fine grooves etched deep and crisscrossing over her beautiful face, sliding up her cheekbone and around her painted mouth. The makeup brightens everything. The rouge is the color of bougainvillea, and the lipstick shines glossy red. She has powdered her face so all the colors blend like a magnificent sunset. She has bathed in petals of eau de toilette and she has crowned her look with a pair of oversized tinted eyeglasses. Lola Ashang is smiling at me like a movie star.

When I go to Lolas' House [*she pushes the plastic frames up the bridge of her nose*], I fix myself up. I put on a little lipstick. If I have the money, I buy myself some powder, an eyeliner and some blush. I'm different than the other old ladies because I like to look good, why not? [*She pinches her nose.*] Many people say if you're old you smell like dirt. So what, I say. Don't we come from earth? They say the old ones smell bad—okay—let's smell everyone together so we can see who smells soiled and old. Not me.

[*She tilts her head at the camera, flirting with the lens.*] I'm not like the others. I change my clothes. I get dressed up and make myself pretty and if they gossip about me, I don't care. It means I'm popular. And you know, that's what I think too about the struggle. Let them talk about us, let them gossip. The whole world needs to know what happened to the women.

After seven months imprisoned in Fort Santiago, my mother-in-law came with her friend, a Japanese reverend. They came to me, and speaking in English, they made some kind of agreement, but I couldn't understand them. All I knew was soon I was walking out the door and down the steps of Fort Santiago. My mother-in-law brought me back to Santa Potenciana.

During my first night of freedom, I soaked in the tub for the first time since my capture. I closed my eyes and I let the water cover me and as I was scrubbing my body, I thought it was strange that I had not menstruated in months. How long has it been, I thought, three months?

In the next few days, my mother-in-law began to receive visitors in our home. The Japanese would give my mother-in-law a sack of rice, or a bundle of fish, or meat, or soap, and she would hand me over to our guests—and in this way the soldiers continued to rape me. Oh, I thought, yun pala, that's why it was so easy to walk out of that garrison. My mother-in-law would steal away while I was with the men and sell the rations for cash so she could gamble all that money away.

One day, when I was scrubbing the stairs, I thought about my body, how it was growing fat. Looking up the wooden staircase, I thought about the child, was it a child? Then, standing up I ran to the top of the steps and threw myself down. When this did not work, I began drinking herbs to abort the baby. Afterward, my stomach ached and when I went to the bathroom, I felt something leaving my body. Staring in the bowl, I saw bright red blood. Ay, thanks, I whispered to myself, I hope it's okay now. Because if I let it be born, then what would my life be like? It's not like I knew who the father was because many had raped me.

When I told my mother-in-law, the old woman nodded and mixed together a concoction of leaves of sambong, alagaw, and guava. She boiled it all together and offered it to me. "Drink this medicine," she told me.

One night after I had recovered, Manong Romero, my husband's cousin, asked me, "What now, Ashang?"

"I will get out of here," I answered.

"But what if you are caught?"

There was a fire escape out the window of our apartment. Across the street, a Japanese soldier kept guard. One night, when he was sleeping, I climbed down the fire escape in a long black dress. Below, a pet monkey was making noise, stirring the guard in his sleep. I froze. I waited. And then I crept down silently, reaching the streets and running directly to the church in San Antonio. There, the sacristan took me in until the morning.

The next day, I snuck onto a calesa and rode to Barrio Obrero, to my uncle's house. As we were on the way, the horse-drawn carriage passed a small carenderia just as they were opening. So I stepped into the restaurant.

"What do you want?" asked the owner.

"A job," I answered. "You don't have to pay me, just as long as I can eat."

Aling Ciony and Mang Felix, the owners of the restaurant took pity on me and took me on as if I were their own child.

I worked there for several weeks, serving tables in the front, when one night a group of Japanese soldiers came into the carenderia. As I was bringing an order to one of the tables, one of the Japanese pointed me out. I dropped my tray and scattered food everywhere. I ran out the back of the restaurant, right into a Chinese cemetery. The graveyard was open, no fences, no gates. I ran and could hear someone chasing after me. The Japanese followed me.

As I stepped across the cemetery, I came upon an open grave and leapt right into it. Naku, Evelina, my whole body was breathing hard. I hid in that grave, covering myself up with fronds and soil, only my feet stuck out. The soldier pulled me out and into the open air. He raped me until I lost consciousness. Then left me lying among the dead.

That night, the cemetery caretaker, Mang Jose, lifted my body and carried me back to the carenderia. After that incident, I no longer served customers, but was sent to the markets to sell loaves of bread from a pushcart.

Ashang leans past the camera, whispering in my ear, telling me the nasty things that people called her when she first told her story to the press.

We're not only talking money here, we're fighting for our dignity. Here in the Philippines there are many gossip mongers. Once when I was interviewed, I came out and I heard a woman say, "How dare she! She's already old and she has the guts to tell her rotten secrets?" I couldn't control myself. You know what I did? I got out of the van and I went right up to her and I said, "Why, what's your problem? Why are you talking about me?" She kept silent. "You weren't raped by the Japanese," I said. "So you're the ugly one!"

I met my second husband shortly after the war ended. He was a Manila officer and one day, I was running through the market, on my way to Pedro Guevara, near the railway, by the Chinese noodle shop.

"Sir," I said to him, "help me. The Japanese are following me."

The policeman looked and then he said, "There's no one following you."

"Where are you going?" I asked him.

"You want to come with me?"

I nodded.

"Even if you don't know me?"

"Yes. Besides I have nowhere else to go."

So I went with him to a hotel at the corner of Ascarraga and Avenida. We fell in love. After I gave birth to our first child, his wife came to me. I was scandalized. But how was I to know? So I left him, taking our child with me to Grace Park where I worked for a Chinese restaurant owner.

You know, he followed me. And then, he begged me to return. He said he'd leave his wife for me.

"You don't know my life," I answered. "You don't know what happened to me in the garrison."

But he insisted I go back to him. "I won't leave you," he told me.

When we had our second child, his wife died and then he asked me to marry him. I wouldn't. I didn't love him. And I was already married once. Together, we had eight children. When he had a stroke, I cared for him for nine years until the day he died. I worked at Aling Cora's, running numbers for Jai-Alai. That's where I met Chiquito. He was an actor. I didn't know what I was doing was wrong, but my children's father wasn't working. So

Chiquito and I went into business. We rented a house and while the children were studying, we sold women. Yes. That's how I was able to raise my eight children by myself.

Fifty years after the war, I saw Lola Rosa and Nelia Sancho on the television. Lola Rosa said to those who listened, those who were victims during Japanese time, during the Second World War, please come over. She said we should all come together. Please don't be ashamed. Don't be afraid.

I said, should I come out? I thought, where do I go? I don't know these television stations. So what I did was, I asked my daughter. Her husband came to me and said, "We're here Lola." He said it like that. "You might want to come out. Ate Tuding is inviting you." Tuding is my sister-in-law and she's already come out. Do you know Tuding? She was the speaker for us. Gertrude Balisalisa. When we came out, she was one of us. Now she's with Malaya. The first one to come out was Lola Rosa, and after a month, my sister-in-law Gertrude, then myself. So, we arrived at the office of Nelia Sancho and I saw one lola there—Amonita. There, that makes four of us. And then, we were always together with Nelia. She took us to give interviews at different stations. Nelia would fetch me here and we'd ride in an air-conditioned taxi and afterward, the two of us would eat at Jollibee. At that time our lawyer was Attorney Capulong. We filed a suit against the Japanese government on April 2, 1993. There were eighteen lolas. At first I was ashamed, you know, to say I was raped and to tell the story, but then again, it was the truth. It's what happened.

After that we were offered a private fund by the Japanese. Yes, the Asian Women's Fund. "I'm going to take it," Rosa told me. "Who knows about tomorrow? How long we will live or if soon we will be dead?" I was just to see my doctor too and he gave me five prescriptions I could not fill. So, I accompanied Lola Rosa to the Japanese embassy and filed for the Asian Women's Fund.

We met officials from the Japanese embassy on my birthday, August 15, 1996. So now we went to the Hyatt Hotel. We could not get in because the reporters were fighting to take our pictures. When they learned it was my birthday, they bought noodles for long life and we celebrated!

Everyone was lined up. Everyone greeted us. "Good day, ma'am!" they said, Uy! It was such a nice feeling. Nelia was not there. You know why? She did not want us to accept the money! But we decided to take it because of our health—we might get sick and have no money for the hospital, or we might die and how will they bury us? That was Lola Rosa's reasoning too!

And now, nothing! During our time—you know we came out first—we were still strong. I said even if we get a mountain of money, it is not enough for the dignity that we've lost during the war. Just think of it, my children have pride, too.

And it's not only that. I was insulted by my friends, my neighbors. That's what happened. When I went out of the house with Nelia, I heard them talking behind my back! And they looked at me. So what I say, even if you give me a mountain of money, it is not enough for the lost dignity of the Filipina. You ask. You have lolas. You have mothers. My story is true.

In October 2008, I sit in my parents' dining room, screening footage from last year's trip to Manila, when Carmen, my two-year-old niece, pops her head around the corner, her eyes bright and her hair swinging in all directions. "What's that?" she wants to know. She has heard the lolas' carnival-like music and it has drawn her to me. She crawls onto a dining room chair and she claps as Lola Ashang dances on the computer screen. The old woman stretches her palms open, flat to the sky as if she is holding it up. Her shoulders pump up and down. She bites her bottom lip as she lifts each leg and stomps to the beat. Her head moves side to side, shifting with the song. A beautiful old marionette with brightly painted cheeks, eyebrows drawn in dark and high like two exclamation points bending to the wind and lips tinted red like tulip petals, Lola Ashang dances while the other women sit at the edge of the patio, talking quietly among themselves. Shiny beads swing across her buxom chest and from her wrists the bangles glitter like stars. Carmen loves it—the music and the little dancing lola and when she sees me enter the frame, towering over Lola Ashang, she claps even louder and yells, "Auntie! Auntie!" On the screen I take hold of Lola Ashang's small hands and we spin to the mandolin, we stomp to the bass drum, we swing our hips to the tambourine, and Carmen giggles and squeals.

That afternoon I play the video segment for Carmen over and over again and every time I do, Carmen's face lights up. "Yoya Ashang!" she calls out, pointing and waving and blowing kisses. With each screening, my niece gets closer to the small figure until her eyelashes brush up against the monitor like kisses. The music stops and Carmen rises off the chair, shouting, "Again, again, again!" fast and furious as if she is afraid that I might walk away and let the image of Lola Ashang fade to black and slip away forever.

Asian Women's Fund

IN 1995, PRIVATE citizens and businesses of Japan created the Asian Women's Fund to atone for the women's suffering during World War II.

The fund was controversial, and while LILA Pilipina supported the women's right to accept the fund, many of the Filipina survivors declined, waiting for the true apology and reparations from the Japanese government. One survivor, Lola Juanita Jamot, accepted the funds. She also wrote a public statement on September 7, 1996. In it, she describes not only her testimony of what happened to her during World War II, but also the reasons why she accepted the funds. She wrote:

> Last August, I accepted the money from Asian Women's Fund. I accepted the money out of necessity. I am poor and dependent on the support of LILA Pilipina and other people for my daily needs. I live alone and have no family to support me.
>
> But despite my acceptance of the AWF, I will continue to demand state compensation and official apologies from the Japanese government. I know the Asian Women's Fund does not give me the justice that I deserve. The Asian Women's Fund does not fulfill the Japanese government's legal responsibility to me and other "comfort women" survivors. The Asian Women's Fund is not state compensation. I have also read Prime Minister Ryutaro Hashimoto's letter, and I know that it is not an official apology from the Japanese government; it is only a personal apology from Mr. Hashimoto.

Learning to Meditate

Pasong Tamo Extension, Makati City, Metro Manila
Wednesday, May 8, 2002

ON WEDNESDAYS, I climb aboard the white school bus with Sister Mary John and we drive through the neighborhoods to pick up one of the Sisters of the Poor along with her charges. We travel to a building on Pasong Tamo Extension in Makati City. The first floor is a bank. When we enter, we greet the security guard and step onto the elevator and hit P for penthouse. When the doors open, we are in the meditation center.

I sit on a simple white folding chair. The meditation teacher looks so familiar to me. She looks a little like a Galang auntie, or maybe my best friend in Chicago. She looks a little like Lorraine, the desk assistant in the local gym I go to in Ermita. Anyway, it's like I've always known her.

Today she tells us we are going to focus on the power of silence. That's a good one, I think. Most days, Manila is so magulo—chaotic with noise—its horns beeping, jackhammers breaking concrete, vendors calling out, and text messages dinging from pedestrian phones. I am living in the city of noise. And then, of course, I am also living with the voices of the lolas. And at night, I dream of their magnificent screams.

I wonder how I will ever find peace.

The trick, she says, is to focus on the light inside. I close my eyes, and there is nothing but darkness and the traffic of a million thoughts. I think there may be a light but it is so small and so dim and the darkness so vast. I nearly miss it for the cloudy film washing over me. And

I wonder: how am I ever going to do this? And as full of doubt as I am, there is a longing to find this silence and witness this so-called light.

We are being asked to breathe deeply. My whole body expands like a rubber balloon. We are being guided to exhale. I let it go, I let it go, I go. I am listening to the sound of my breath and all around me I feel the heat of little candles burning everywhere.

Take time out from thinking, she says.

I breathe in and suddenly all the voices of the lolas are calling me to come and eat. "Evelina!" they call, "Kumain ka na!"

"You are too skinny," they say.

"No, she is too fat," they say.

"She is too single."

"When are you going to marry, na?"

Take a rest from your mind, interrupts the meditation teacher. See your own light.

I have no idea what that means. I keep my eyes closed. I wait.

IT IS LIKE slipping into the ocean and sinking into its darkness. And all around is the sound of water, churning from the surface of the sea. In this space there is only black and the beating of the heart is magnified. Deeper and deeper I fall and there is stillness everywhere.

And just as I am settling in the dark, a light spins like the grooves of a forty-five record. Shoots out in the dark like the weave of finely spun spider webs. The light explodes and I see the tiniest star at the bottom of the sea. Shiny, bright and blue.

URDUJA SAMONTE

Born November 27, 1920,
Lamitan, Basilan, Aklan

Abducted by the Imperial
Japanese Army, 1944, Washington, Aklan

Urduja Is the sweet flesh of kopra

La, what's for tomorrow?
Why, you're going home now?
Not yet, I'm going to take your picture first.
You said you'd stay with me for two days.
I'll be back tomorrow. Do I disappoint you?
No. Tomorrow I will speak English to you, but you are not
an American woman.
No?
Because you are Filipino, that's what . . .
In my heart and in my blood.
Yes. And you are a guerrilla.
Oh no! I am only talking to you. Ay, Lola!
That is what I am telling you about God. You cannot see what
has been planned for you. Can you not see that? You are a
guerrilla, anak.
Oh, Lola. Are you happy?
Yes, I am happy, but if you are no longer here, I have no one
to talk to. So that's it.

—Urduja Samonte, March 11, 2001, Metro Manila

YOUR NAME IS like a witch's chant—Urduja, Urduja, Francisco Samonte. Your skin sans wrinkles, your mouth painted red, and half of your teeth missing. Your wide, flat nose. To sing your name, Urduja Francisco Samonte, summons you and there you are—long thin hair dyed black and pulled into a bun that sits on the crown of your head. Princess Urduja. Warrior Urduja. How many times have you barged into the Lolas' House, hands on hips, slinging words at everyone? You gave the evil eye and your kisses just as freely. It depended on the height of the sun or the figure of the moon. It depended on a clock that only you could read. You were a moody one, old lady, you and your wicked tongue. How many times did you wave your long painted fingernails at me and say, You think you are so smart, Evelina, but I know what you are thinking. I know.

And maybe you did. And maybe you didn't. The point was that you got me to believe that you did. How I loved to taunt you and send your tongue spinning into what you called sitsiritsit [*chi-chi-ritch-ee*]. You told me that if you could, you'd spend all day long sitting on a bench making your stories. Making sitsiritsit. How do I tell your story? How do I get it right?

When I close my eyes and whisper your name, I see you standing there. Your voice, as clear to me as my own, rings and echoes in the chambers of my heart. It is as if you are with me still. And you are speaking my name, chanting, Evelina, do you know this, Evelina? Somehow testing me. I will close my eyes today. I will write your name. I will listen to you, you storyteller, you spell maker, you widow of three husbands. I will show them just who you were, you Muslim Princess, you Christian orphan, you lover of Jose Rizal.

My name is Urduja Francisco Samonte. I was born on November 27, 1920, on the island of Basilan. I was named after the Warrior Princess Urduja. Like my namesake, I have been through so many wars and fought them all without the help of any men, so strong am I that all my tears have dried up. Some days, I am even stronger than Princess Urduja—for I can make kulam on those who are evil. I light a candle, burn it near a likeness of that person, and then there it is—a heart attack, a pain in the side, a lesson to stay honest. Nothing gets past me. And like the warrior princess, it seems that no one hears me when I talk. No

202

one listens to me, Evelina. They think I am full of sitsiritsit—bullshit. But I know what I am talking about. I know things now in my eighty years that I didn't know back then.

We are sitting in your sala, and you are talking about everything but the past.

"So Lola," I say, my fingers rubbing at your leg.

"Some days, I am too tired you know."

"But La, I came from so far away. Just tell me again."

You take a swig from the bottle of Red Bull. You settle back, and closing your eyes, you talk.

These days, I wake up weak. The leukemia holds my body down, close to the earth, draining my color. Some days I take two doves and I drink their blood, as if lovebirds can bring me back. That is an old witch's trick. But even those tricks fail me these days. I've put kulam on both Philippine and U.S. presidents, and still they are up and running. I breathe the air. It is hot and sticky, but it is air. I no longer have the energy to tell you the story again. Don't you have it? From your first visit when I came to the Lolas' House, when you interviewed the fifteen of us? Don't you have it yet? Can't we speak French instead?

"Gyera, Gyera!" That is what they'd say to us. War is coming. What is Gyera? We didn't know what they meant. Even as my uncle took us into the forest of Dumagit to hide among the trees, evacuating our village and abandoning our houses, what did we understand of that word? Of the Japanese? We didn't know what they looked like, much less who they were.

My girl cousins and I hid in the woods, along with so many of our villagers. We spent the days under the shade of palm branches, in the hollows of trees, lying on wet grass and gathering the buwa, the sweet round fruit in the shell of the kopra. I was a widow at seventeen. I was the illegitimate child of a Muslim soldier and a Christian teenager. Abandoned by mother and orphaned by my father. How much worse could this war be, Evelina?

One day, Siling, Lucien, and I were napping when my tomboy cousin Christine snuck up behind us and whispered, "Tara, tara!" She wanted us to go with her, take long sticks and stab at the green husks, open them up and suck on the sweet juice of coconut. She climbed over us and lured us deep into the wood. The other villagers gathered the kopra for the trucks, harvested them for the money, but we were hungry and young, not thinking of the future, only our stomachs. So we stabbed at the husks and we broke open the shells and the juice trickled down our chins, cool and milky. The sun weaved in between the forest trees, hitting spots on the earth, lighting fallen kopra. The others gathered the fruit in silence. It was so quiet, we could hear the earth breathing.

And then, Evelina, in the middle of the woods, we heard voices echoing against the trunks of trees. "Everyone come out!" yelled the voices. "Everyone come out!" The whole village stopped, froze like children in the middle of a game. And the voice that we heard was angry and it seemed to fall from the skies like heavy stones. "If you don't come out, huwes de kutsilyo!"

"What is huwes de kutsilyo?" everyone asked. But the voice, which spoke our native tongue, continued to warn us, to demand we make ourselves known. Do you know what is huwes de kutsilyo, Evelina? It is justice by the knife. They were going to take all the people they had captured and kill them if we did not come out. Huwes de kutsilyo. And do you know who was calling us? Our own people who had betrayed us, the Makapili! Filipino spies!

This must be war, then. This was it? The leaves of the palms began to move, to brush against our legs, and bodies and the shadows began to dance in and out of the woods, and people came out of hiding. One by one, they came forward. And then, as if the wind blew through that whole forest and placed us in the middle of a monsoon storm, gunshots flew into the sky. The villagers ran fast, leaping from trees, falling from all corners of the wood, and we could not discern where they were going. The Japanese ran into the forest to flush the rest out, shooting their guns, hitting stones, barreling into trees. Every now and then shots fired into a leg or deep into a shoulder and so now everyone was running and calling out to God, "What did we do?" It was like the whole world was screaming to get out of their bodies.

Our mouths were still full and wet with coconut milk. I chewed the sweet flesh of the buwa and thought of the day enemies ambushed my father. I was only twelve years old when he died. I knew I could bear anything, at least that's what I thought. My cousins and I snuck around the trees, moved in the opposite direction, going deeper into the woods.

We hung kopra shells around our necks, slung them over our shoulders. As we walked, the kopra knocked one against the other and rang soft as chimes. Soon, we saw an opening. We heard a truck coming down the road, believing it was the kopra truck. We waited, still peeling at the kopra, still sucking on the fibers. As the truck approached we realized that the truck had been captured and was being driven by the Japanese. The truck carried people from our barrio. They stopped and jumping from the trucks, they pointed their bayonets at us, tried to grab us, but we ran, dropping the kopra everywhere. Shells rolled under the feet of the Japanese, made them trip into the jungle, nearly falling on their own swords and this only made them angrier. We ran and ran. We ran. They surrounded us—Siling, Christine, Lucien, and me. They kicked us. They shoved us. They poked us with the sharp end of their bayonets. They rolled us to the foot of the truck and waved their arms up, crying, "Kura! Kura!" We did not know "kura, kura." I wanted to fight, but how can you fight when you don't have a gun? Our beautiful buwa scattered on the ground before us, crushed under the weight of the trucks' wheels. Is this it, you wonder? Oh no, Evelina, not yet. Listen.

When the truck came to the main road, we saw thousands of people from the neighboring towns all lined up and ready to march from Dumagit to New Washington. There were miles and miles of people, Evelina. Old and young and entire families. My mother and cousins were there. I could not stop weeping as we began the long march to New Washington.

The sun was so hot that day and there was no shade for us. We had to walk and walk. And as we did the Japanese taunted us with their guns, hitting us with the back end of the gun, poking us with the bayonet. When the old people grew too weak to walk, they shoved them with their feet, they spat on them. Of course, when you're old, you walk slowly, so then they bayoneted the old. When the children cried too loud and faltered in their step, the soldiers slapped them over the head. Sinipa sila! HMMM! Sometimes they shot gunfire through the crowds to scare everyone to move faster. I thought to myself, this is it. We're dead. We walked what felt like hours. The hot sun took all the water from our bodies, left our throats parched and our tongues dry.

I have no idea how far we walked, but by five in the afternoon, the long line of people had reached New Washington. I could see all the people in the plaza lined up and waiting. There were many, many people there from so many other barrios. Too many to count all of them. The Japanese had gathered all our people like they were collecting coins, pooling us all together like that, then counting us and dividing us into groups.

The garrison was inside the compound of a coconut plantation surrounded by barbed wire. The gates we walked through were made of bamboo. From the plaza we could see the main building, the plantation owner's house. You know, Evelina, that guy gave his house to the Japanese—he was a collaborator, a Makapili! All along the compound, Japanese soldiers stood guard, holding their long bayonets up in the air, ready to attack.

And then they started to divide us. It made me even more scared when they separated all of us.

Old people over here!

Men over there!

Families here!

And all the women, they put inside—everyone else stayed outside, but they put us in the basement of a kopra warehouse.

They didn't speak to us—but threw us one by one into one of three rooms. I counted twenty-five women in my room. There were no chairs. No beds. No rugs to sleep on, only the cold floor. We sat there on the floor, our knees drawn to our chests, our faces covered in sweat and dirt, and we stared at one another, not talking, not knowing what to do. Since they had gathered people from several barrios, we were not accustomed to the faces before us, and this made me even more nervous.

We could hear screaming from outside our room and some noises. I leaned on our thin wooden wall and listened. The wall was made of soft cheap wood. If I pressed my finger hard enough I could make an impression. Someone poked a small hole and we could see more women on the other side. Twenty-five of them. We took turns looking into the hole, as if we might recognize someone there, as if seeing them might bring us help. But do you know what it is to look through a hole as big as your finger and only see yourself looking back? It was a cage of wood—without any windows except a small one with bars. If we wanted to look outside, we had to climb on the tops of each other's shoulders, just to get to the light. But when we got to the top of the window, all we saw was more death. In the plaza, they would line civilians up and execute them.

They had no mercy, Evelina. They'd slice the pregnant women's bellies open and yank the baby from the womb. They'd take their hands and rip the cord from the mother and child. Then they take that baby and they toss him high to the sky and make a game of skewering newborn infants on the tips of their swords. So many babies tossed in the air that way. So many of them caught on the sharp end of a bayonet. That is how they were.

That first night, Evelina, here it was. Ito na. HMMMP! The Japanese entered our room. Not caring where they were, they'd choose a girl and rape her right there on the floor in front of all of us. Two Japanese came at me at one time, each one pulling on an arm. I could feel my skin slipping out of me, I could feel my body gliding out of hands and sliding into the sweaty uniform of another. Naku! You would not even believe it!

I fought. HMMMP! I kicked and I squirmed even as they were fighting over me. The sword slashed my wrist. Comere, you give me your hand, anak, I will show you. Can you feel the wound here?

I trace the shape of the scar on your wrist, a little crescent moon. A tiny heat, a memory of that first night. You yank my hand to another injury. I feel an egg-sized lump on the wing of your shoulder. Then what happens next: you unbutton your pants and let them slip off your wide hips, turning to show me your backside. The camera keeps rolling.

"Give me your hand," you say, "I want you to see this—this is when they threw me down, I couldn't even get up. Can you feel this?"

"Opo, Lola," I say, sighing. "I feel it."

"I don't want to cry anymore, Evelina."

"Yes, Lola."

I search the length of your back, walking my fingers where your tailbone meets the spine. A bone juts out of place, jagged as the tip of a bayonet. I take a deep breath.

"There is another wound on my face, over here," you say.

I mark the scar with the palm of my hand. The skin is rough like it has never healed.

"And over here, Evelina, on my throat. It's small now right? Maliit, di ba?"

"Opo," I say, "maliit na." It feels small but hard, like a pebble under your skin.

"Naku, Evelina. The second soldier who raped me he threw me down. HMMMP! Like that. I can still smell the stink of his cigarette, puffing smoke in the dingy room and all the voices crying, 'HUWAG! HUWAG! No,' they shouted. And then he ripped my dress up here."

You open up your blouse and lift your breasts to the camera.

What do you think, I am going to hide my wounds? He took his hands and put them here. And I am thinking, Oh God why do you make me live so long? And he says, Oh nice like pussy! And he takes his cigarette and he puts it out between my breasts. Then he puts his face here and he smells! Can you imagine, he used me like an ashtray! My breasts were bleeding and raw and still he rubbed his moustache there.

I dislocated my back, I broke my leg. After my third month, they stopped using me because I had venereal disease. Ay, Evelina, thank God, because of this V.D., they sent me to Lola Bilay, an old Filipina who was thought to be a Makapili. She fed us and

she took care of us, and actually, she was a Filipina spy working for the guerrillas. You know guerrillas, right? Filipinos fighting for Filipinos. She took the bark of the malunggay tree, mixed it with root of coconut, and she put the soothing mix on my sores.

It was the only time I got any rest.

For seven months, the soldiers raped me day and night. Not one, not two, not three, but many, many Japanese. Sometimes ten, sometimes fifteen. Sometimes the same soldier would rape five girls in a row.

If we were not locked up in the wooden cell, they'd take us out to watch the executions. You think you're going for a nice walk to feel the sun, maybe step your tired feet into the cool river and take a bath. But they'd take us to the river and we would watch civilians dig a hole in the ground and when the hole was deep enough, the Japanese sliced the heads off those civilians and their bodies would collapse as their heads fell into the holes. Or sometimes, the Japanese would shoot a line of people and make others dig their graves and then they'd make them carry the dead to the grave. After prisoners placed their countrymen in the graves, the soldiers would shoot and the prisoners would also fall into the grave. That is how they treated us, Evelina.

When I was almost healthy already, Lola Bilay helped me escape! On this night, most of the Japanese soldiers went to the town of Estancia and left only a few of the soldiers here. So Lola Bilay gave us a signal and my cousin Siling, another woman named Tessie, and I crawled our way through the floor to the ground. We climbed over the barbed-wire fence. The fence was so high and full of metal thorns and as I was reaching for the ground, my thigh tore on the barb wire and I saw blood flowing, but I did not stop. I did not feel my skin cut open, I did not feel the pain of the wound. I only knew I was leaving.

The night was so dark, and I could hear the river moving through the earth. We walked toward the water and met two of Lola Bilay's guerrilla friends who rowed us across to malaking bayan. After we crossed the river, the three of us parted and I never saw Tessie or Siling again.

There are days when I hear all the whispering. I turn around fast and I stare at the place where the voices are coming from, but I cannot stop the voices. Soon after the war, the voices haunted me and I lost myself for ten years. I cannot remember what I did back then. I cannot remember who I was. Only that my mother sent me away on vacation.

"But where will I vacation?" I asked her.

"Go to Manila," she said.

And in the meanwhile, I could hear the neighborhood whisper, Tira ng Hapones! Tira ng Hapones. Like I wanted to be used by the Japanese. Like I want to be anyone's leftover, much less the Japanese's.

For ten years after the war, nawala ako sa sarili ko! Because all my life, the whispering makes circles in my head. Even as a child, in the womb of my beautiful Christian mother, I heard them whispering. No, it can't be—no you mustn't. Even then, nobody wanted me. My father was a Muslim soldier—he was not supposed to fall in love with her. He was not supposed to touch her—but what can you do when you are two young and beautiful people like they were? What does love know of Islam and Christianity? It knows no difference—only feelings and beauty—and what it means to hold someone you love. I am a result of that love. But they were never allowed to be together. They got married on the condition that they would never be together—if I were a boy I would go with her and if I were a girl, I would go with him.

She never wanted me. Soon as I was born, she left me and started a new life as a single lady. It was my father who loved me. It was my lolo, my father's father. It was my beautiful spinster tita. They treated me like the warrior princess I was— but still there was the whispering. I was never good enough for anyone.

And when my father died, and then my lolo and then my aunt, I was forced to live with my mother's mother. I was treated like a slave, made to do all the work and never doing it to their liking. Whispering and whispering always following me everywhere I go.

Di ko kaya, Evelina. I have no more tears. Even the old ladies at Lolas' House whisper secrets about me. Secrets that are not true. But you, Evelina, you love me anyway. You ask to see me. You ask to hear my story. You don't seem to mind that some-times I am funny, and sometimes my body is so old and losing life so quickly, I cannot be bothered to even look at you.

Do you know what it's like to be whispered about? To walk into a room and for the room to go silent? To be called names on the street and sent away from your home because your mother doesn't want you, doesn't understand you, and finally, is so ashamed of you? I will tell you what it's like. I will tell you because you keep asking me, holding me, kissing me. I think you really want to know. I think you'll let them see me as I am.

What is it that you want, Evelina? Why are you so bound and determined to tell this story? You are not one of us. I can tell from the way you carry your body—like it is a candle and you must keep it very straight so as not to burn everything in sight. You are so intelligent, but I see you are holding back. Something is lacking. Perhaps a spiritual healing. I will tell you something, Evelina. If you put your trust in the Lord, He will keep you alive a long time, He will make you so strong, you will outlive all your companions. But to me, you move not with your heart, but your head. Not with your spirit but your intellect. And even so, some-thing is pushing you to come here. I know if you wanted to, you could spend your days with your family. But you come here, you stay with us—what makes you do that?

Urduja, Urduja, Urduja Samonte. Urduja, Urduja Francisco Samonte. Lola, don't you know, I am right here.

Nawala ako sa sarili ko. I lost myself to myself. I could not find me even as I was here, inside me. For ten years, you went mad. Lost your-self to yourself, your spirit swam in an abyss of whispers and taunts. All you remember is being sent to Manila, but what happened after that? When did you lose yourself? In the middle of that first night of your garrison life? In that moment when your mother sent you away? When did you start to forget yourself, Urduja, Urduja, Urduja Samonte?

Married at the age of sixteen, your attorney husband won a big case, had a few drinks on his way home that night, ran the car into a tree. I asked you, "Anong nangyari, Lola? What happened?" And you looked at me blankly, said, "Wala, patay. Nothing. Dead."

Suddenly, in 1951 you watch the Miss Philippines contest and see a town mate on the stage, a beauty that you once were, or recognized. She brought you home, made you see your own self. Hindi ka nawala sa sarili mo. Somehow she got you to go back to Mindanao, somehow she brought you to your second husband, the beautiful mestizo who was half white and half Filipino. He would be the father of your only daughter. You remember that, you remember going back home to Basilan after that.

You tell me you had three husbands, that you enjoyed their bodies, but there was no love. Really, Lola? The second one died in a car crash, too. You were having your miracle baby at that time, your over-forties baby. Your third husband was an older man, a clean man, well groomed and handsome, he was a good companion. Again, you insist, "Of course man and woman must lie side by side, must have sex, but there was no feeling like love." How much of this has to do with what happened to you back there in the garrisons of New Washington?

Perhaps your body was so damaged there was no feeling left. Maybe there was nothing left but habit. And so sex came easy for you. One husband could replace another. One friend in exchange for another. And the one place the Japanese soldiers could not touch was your heart. Maybe this has something to do with it. You can still feel that place inside of you where your light is very bright and full of wit. You can still protect that place. And all these eighty years, you have kept the heart a sacred space, free from men.

From the first day I met you, Lola Urduja, you have told me your story, and I cannot believe that no one has heard you say it. I cannot believe that all the times you stood before the Japanese embassy, the U.S. embassy, and Malacañang Place, you and the lolas holding up your signs and shouting your transgressions, nobody was listening. Each month you waited to hear what the appeals court of Japan would have to say about the terrible tales you have revealed. And the answer each month was no answer at all. And now the years are taking each of you.

I see you, sometimes when I sleep. I see you when I am in the blue Atlantic Ocean, trying to wrap myself in the safety of those salty waves. I lift my arms up to the sun and let the water rush over my skin, and I can feel the weight of your arms in my hands, the shape of a dislocated spine bulging underneath your soft skin. So many wounds are in the nerves of my fingertips. So many memories of your life are running in my skin's memory. I let the ocean lift my legs, carry me yards from the shore, and I am reminded of how the soldiers would lift you up and slam you on the basement floor.

In these moments at the sea, I wonder how you could have kept your sense of humor, all those years. How in the middle of the interview you'd turn to me and say, "Do you know what that is, Evelina? I am speaking French. Do you know French?" How despite the horrible things that happened to you in the war, you still knew the value of the body—how to hold one, to touch one, to have sex with one. Three husbands?

I wonder how many weeks you waited after I left you that March 2002, how long it took before you actually passed away. I wonder how you died—if you drifted out of your body in your sleep or if your death was something big and dramatic like the days when you peeled your clothes off to reveal all your war wounds. Stepping before the camera, you'd reveal parts of your body, your image looming out of focus and your voice crying in heavy groans.

What is it that I want? I hear your story and I know I am responsible for what I know. I know I should be listening, hearing, writing down your words, joining you and the lolas, fighting for justice. But I am one woman.

Oh, Lola Urduja. The legend of Princess Urduja, a woman warrior, who fought so many battles was doubted. Nobody believed such a woman could exist. There are some who say she is part of Pangasinan history; there are other scholars who say she is a Pangasinan myth.

Urduja, Urduja, Urduja Samonte. I am chanting your name to show you once and for all, I hear you and I know who you are. Surrounded by your tough exterior, once you open up, you are the sweet flesh of kopra. And I? I hear you speaking so clearly and I know now that you are right. I am a guerrilla.

Coercion

WALKING OUT OF an English Department meeting, my colleague Frank asks me if I have heard what Prime Minister Abe has said.

"Don't get me started," I answer. "I have a lot of work to do."

I'm junior faculty getting ready to go on leave and am expected to write a book and publish it if I want to keep my job. So no, I don't want to know what he said, but I do know. The prime minister of Japan has told the world that there is not enough evidence to prove the women have been coerced.

Later that week, my friend Natalie and I sit in her jeep in the parking lot of a grocery store and she asks me, too, "What are you going to do about it, Evey?"

What am I to do? And yet for one week I think about something that the filmmaker Dai Sil Kim-Gibson once said, "Once you hear the stories, your body will not sit still."

And even as I try my best to ignore the news, I find myself staying up late at night, trolling the Internet, reading the headlines. I try writing all the major newspapers. I do my best to tell the *New York Times* and the *Washington Post* that I have seen the evidence. I have touched the evidence.

Nobody answers my emails.

So I begin a blog, *Laban for the Lolas*, and I write about the lolas.

In this way, Annabel Park finds me and I begin to work with her and Eric Byler on the 121 Coalition. Congressman Mike Honda has authored House Resolution 121, and that bill asks Japan to apologize to the lolas and all "comfort women" they have captured and brutalized.

I take a break from writing. I lobby with Annabel and Eric. We put our talents together and cut a short public announcement where we share Dolor Molina's testimony at Emilio Jacinto Elementary School in Tondo, Metro Manila.

In Florida, my students and I travel around the community, reading women's testimonies out loud at parks, and schools, and other civic gatherings. We bring stacks of blank paper and at the end of each reading we ask the audience to write their congressman or woman and tell them to support H.Res. 121.

In Washington, I visit my congresswoman, Ileana Ros-Lehtinen. She is the highest ranking Republican on the House Committee on Foreign Affairs. Once she signs on to the bill, she encourages other Republicans to join her.

By July 30, 2007, Congress meets and passes House Resolution 121 unanimously. And that bill makes way for similar bills from other nations—and still the Japanese government remains silent.

Perhaps I should stick to the writing of books. But I cannot not help myself. I cannot not stay quiet. I find myself moving, speaking, writing, lobbying.

I sit high in the balcony of the House of Representatives on the day of the vote. I watch each congressperson stand. I listen to the vote. I think to myself, if nothing else, their stories are now on record. Their voices have been heard.

CARMENCITA COSIO RAMEL
Mansion at San Miguel, Bulacan
June 14, 2002

Born November 22, 1926,
Los Banos, Laguna

Abducted by the Imperial
Japanese Army, April 1944,
San Miguel, Bulacan

The Mansion of Bulacan

ABANDONED LONG AGO, the three-story house was once a mansion. Green paint has faded and peeled from its exterior and the lattice windows have broken panes, but you can still see that this was once a rich family's home. Intricate wooden carvings border the windows. Scallop trim hangs from the roof and the delicate cupola at the top of the house. Eight-foot-tall cement posts guard the property entrance. Now, the building is in decay. There are iron bars on all the windows. When you peek in, there is nothing but cement and the remnants of walls. It is barren in there. It is haunted.

On this trip to San Miguel, Bulacan, Lola Carmencita Ramel barely speaks at all. Her eyes, big and brown, hold tears in them. I have yet to see the tears fall. But as she walks the grounds, I see she has gone back.

One day in May of 1944, my parents sent me to the center of town to buy some things. I left my house to go shopping in San Miguel. I remember it was our summer season because the corn was tall. I knew the Japanese soldiers were in San Miguel.

On my way there I met three women about my age, nineteen, and I decided to walk with them because I felt lonely. The footpath we walked was surrounded by tall cogon grass. Halfway to San Miguel ten Japanese soldiers hiding in the grasses came running to us. They dragged us into the brush, grabbing our clothes at the arms and breast and shouting, "Kura! Kura!"

I resisted them and I tried to escape, but they punched me in the stomach with their fists until I lost consciousness.

I walk that same path with her. The grass is dry from too much sun. We pass a carabao submerged in mud. His tail swats flies and his head rises above the thick dark bath. "He's trying to cool himself," she tells me. There is no breeze and no respite from the heat, except for when we stop under the shade of a big tree. "They took me here," she tells me. "The Japanese." I reach my hand out to her arm and squeeze.

When I recovered I found myself brought back to the house that they turned into their barracks. It was a three-story private home. They grabbed me by the hair and threw me into one of the rooms. I could see a Japanese soldier sitting at a table in another room. I was with the three girls.

The moment they pushed us into this room the ten Japanese soldiers attacked us. They used the butt of their rifles to beat me on the feet and knees to keep me from walking away or resisting them. After that each of us was raped by all of them. I became so weak that I stopped resisting and I let them do what they wanted to do while I wept and wept. Eventually, I lost consciousness again. When I woke I was lying in the room with the three other girls.

What did she think when she woke up in that room in this house? A beautiful Spanish mansion. The walls would have been intact then. The ceilings high and windows gleaming in capiz. "I was too weak to fight them," she tells me.

The space haunts me. On the one hand it is empty and dark, but on the other, I can see the soldier. He is, as Lola Carmencita has reported, walking back and forth, the rifle on his shoulder, the footsteps clear and precise. There is an image of the girls watching from an open door. The beautiful room has been relieved of all its furniture. Nothing remains but the girls. Along the walls lattice windows with magnificent panes of capiz pull open. Once, Lola Carmencita, says, she was able to sneak a peek out the window. Countless soldiers milled about the grounds.

For the first few days, the girls boycotted food. Every time the Japanese brought a tray of pumpkin mash, the girls looked away. Each day they grew weaker until eventually, they had to eat.

Where did you bathe? I ask her. Where did you relieve yourselves?

She only looks at me with those eyes and the near-falling tears. She points into the room.

On the third day, the soldiers came to our room to rape us again and one of the girls ran toward the door to escape. The soldier ran after her, grabbed her by the hair and stabbed her in the vagina with his bayonet. She fell down and bled everywhere. Again I lost consciousness. When I woke up there were only three of us left.

Even after the incident, the Japanese soldiers kept on raping us during the afternoon, day by day. About one week passed after we had been detained. One day I woke up and realized the other women had disappeared from the room. I couldn't understand why and how they had left me there. After a while, there were fewer Japanese. Then they stopped bringing me food. They stopped raping me. And finally, I was left alone. I was so weak I could not get up. I was lying in the room for a few days and finally a few Filipino civilians looked through the window. When they saw me, they said, "There's someone in there," but they didn't come to get me. Later that day, my mother arrived. She told me she searched for me everywhere and when she heard that this house had been turned into a garrison, she came. I could not walk out of the house. I was too weak. My mother and another Filipino had to help me out.

Outside, I take numerous photographs of her before the building. She looks like a tourist standing before the ruins of Rome. At one point, she curls her fingers around the iron bars of an open window and looks away from the lens.

I hear the crying women. I feel the pounding of that rifle butt on the bottoms of the soles. It is as if I am there, in the past, with them.

The air is still thick with foul energy.

I close my eyes and listen to the cicadas in the trees. I hear the wind pushing branches about.

Today, Lola Carmencita walks the grounds, peering into all the windows of the house, running her hands along the concrete walls. Today, her tears threaten to fall. I watch her figure moving along the border of the house, poking through the iron gates, attempting to get in.

fever

Nursia at St. Scholastica's
Malate, Manila
June 29, 2002

SIXTEEN STORIES AND eight months later, my body rebels. Hours after my last interview with Lola Carmencita, I burn with fever and it's as if I have donned their lives, cloaked my skin in the scent of their tales. I have stepped into their world—houses made of concrete blocks, half-made, half-undone, dark as caves. Or four poles, a floor woven of grass and a thatched roof. A hole in the ground to release human waste. I have sat at the tables as if I were their apo, eating fish and gulay and rice and sour soups.

I have listened and before their words could take me down, I diverted my feelings. I focused on the camera or the noise on the street, I said something about the clamor of children ruining the sound.

But my body heard everything. Lolas constantly rubbed their hands over my arms, my legs. Sniffed at my skin the way my own Lola did so many times. They cast a spell on me, made me love them.

Today I let go the breath that I have been holding. My body sweats, convulses, shits, and vomits for two weeks straight. I spit out all the vile acts committed upon the lolas. The constant raping each night, the sight of fathers being skinned alive, baby brothers being tossed into the air and skewered by bayonets, the insanity of a mother grieving the loss of her child, a woman, scarred, breasts cut off at the height of pregnancy. I spit. I shit. I cry. I burn with fever.

This is what it's like to hold secrets in the vessel of the heart, in the pores of skin, in the limbs of this body. To know it and pretend it doesn't live here. I cannot hold the stories for eight months. My pen

221

flies across the page and cannot spit the words out fast enough to describe all that I have heard.

How much more their bodies, aching with this knowledge? This secret they've held onto for fifty years? How much more the pain and the disease to the body and mind? I cannot help but wonder what the world would do if it knew what I know.

I dream of my own life, and my family and all my beautiful nieces, my students and their students, all the young women I have met who call me Ate, and I am wondering how this legacy of the lolas might become a blessing to our children. Or how, if kept in the dark, it might remain a curse meant only to repeat itself.

"Ano ba ito, Lola?" I ask. "Paano ba ito?"

In my delirium, they stand guard at my bedside. They wrap around the door and into the hallway. They travel down the concrete steps of Nursia and out into the middle of Ermita. One hundred and seventy-three Filipina grannies who have spoken up, thousands more who remained silent, four hundred thousand women in the neighboring countries of Korea, China, Malaysia, Indonesia, and the Dutch East Indies, all speaking now, all whispering the stories and setting themselves free. Paano ba ito, I ask again.

And each of my lolas opens up her arms, wide and not hesitating. She takes me as her own and shows me how to live a life.

"Sa awa ng Diyos, anak, sa awa ng Diyos."

Homecoming

THE SUN COMES through the wall-sized window, casting afternoon light on our family room. Outside the trees sway vibrant and green, shading a small figure of Mama Mary. She welcomes me too with arms stretched and hands waiting. Inside, noise percolates from every room of the house. From my suitcase I pull a salmon-colored tapestry. When you first glance at it, the greens, blues, and reds flash a beautiful montage of color. The folds unwind and reveal the fine embroidery.

I'm telling my mother and sister-in-law that when Lola Remedios learned I was coming to Lolas' House, she began working on this piece as a gift to me. It took her eight months to get this far in the tapestry. Every piece—every letter and image has been cut from other fabrics and painstakingly handsewn into the cloth. Except for the missing D where she has embroidered, "(D)ecember 20, 1942, Dito Ako Nahuli Sa Lugar ng Baryo Esperanza," it's all there—the Daguitan River, green mountains and lush trees, the nipa hut where she grew up. Every piece has been meticulously stitched onto the fabric.

On the top border she has chain-stitched in large green letters:

"My Name is Remedios Felias From the Province of Burauen Leyte Barrio Esperanza And I Was Born On Jan 29, 1928."

The rest of the text scattered across the cloth is in Tagalog. It borders scenes of Lola Remedios as a teenager running through the fields and leaping over barbed-wire fences. She catches her leg on the spur of a fence, and on the fabric there is a trail of red chain stitching. Close behind are soldiers running with their bayonets pointed up to the sky, their legs in a straddled sprint, their white scarves flapping in the wind. One soldier has skewered a baby on his sword. She has sewn two black x's in its tiny face. These are the eyes. Red thread flies from its round form. It is all there, pieced together in a nonlinear montage. She has made tiny Japanese soldiers like paper doll cutouts. She has sewn herself into the lining and stitched her hair wild and black, blood everywhere. It is all there, the capture, the torture, the raping. It is all there, the planes and the white background and red sun of that flag, the garrison and the bars, and her face behind them. It is an astounding work of folk art, it is her testimony.

"Dito Ako Ikinulong."

Here is where I was kept.

She has set her story free on this canvas. She has given it to me so I can bring it with me everywhere I go, so she can speak for herself long after she dies from cancer of the stomach. It is the testimony she has given to the Japanese courts, to the media, and now, to me, in this one-by-three-foot piece of cloth.

I hold the tapestry up and my sister-in-law and mother are just beginning to understand the images when Nina, my niece who has just turned four, walks into the room, says, "What's that?" I fold the piece in two. I tuck it under my arms. Say, "Just a blanket." I lean over and pick up her sippy-cup and coax her into the kitchen. "Want some more milk?" I think the moment is over, that all she had seen was a blur of colors on an old piece of cloth. But then my sister-in-law tells me on the ride back to their home, Nina called out from her car seat, "Mommy, if I am pretty enough, will the soldiers leave you and Daddy alone?"

REMEDIOS FELIAS

Born January 29, 1928,
Burauen Leyte, Barrio Esperanza

Abducted by the Imperial
Japanese Army, December 20, 1942

Lola Remedios and the women of LILA Pilipina dramatize the abduction of a "comfort woman" during a protest at the Japanese embassy June 14, 2002

Justice
by knife

THE DIRECT TRANSLATION of huwes de kutsilyo is justice by knife. It is that moment when the enemy troops slay the earth, the animals, the people.

There is nothing just about it.

When the lolas talk about huwes de kutsilyo they describe a showering of bullets. They hear the thud of brothers, sisters, mothers, and fathers falling heavy to the ground.

The lolas tell you stories of babies thrown up in the air and caught by the end of a bayonet. One lola has images of her father being skinned alive playing over and over. She cannot stop seeing it. She cannot stop.

This then is not justice by the knife.

Huwes de kutsilyo is the most violent moments of war.

An Invitation to Japanese Prime Minister Shinzō Abe

Posted at the *Laban for the Lolas* Website
on the Eve of Women's International Day
March 7, 2007

Dear Prime Minister Shinzō Abe,

You don't know me, but I invite you to meet the women of LILA
Pilipina. On March 2, 2007, you announced, "There is no evidence
to prove there was coercion, nothing to support it (the coercion of
World War II military sex slaves)." I've been working with surviving
World War II "comfort women" of the Philippines since 1998. Let
me take you to Lolas' House, a tiny cottage in Quezon City, Manila
where women meet and gather the evidence you need to prove there
was, indeed, coercion.

If 81-year-old Pilar Frias is there, she will begin by singing to you
her song, "The Life of a 'Comfort Woman.'" And she will tell you that
in 1942 she had two bouts with Japanese soldiers before she was
taken captive. During the first intrusion, soldiers cornered her and
shouted in a foreign tongue. Confused, Pilar didn't react. Frustrated,
a soldier took his cigarette and held it to her face, tipped the lighted
end and burned a hole into her skin. She cried out and the soldier
drew his knife and sliced her nose. Blood poured from her face and as
she cried he yanked her by the hair and shoved her head deep into a
bin of water. The blood blossomed in a cloud of red. The soldiers stole

the family's livestock—a cow, some chickens and pigs. They raided their supply of rice and other dried goods. During the next invasion, they raped her five times—each time it was a different soldier. Seventeen years old and bleeding, they tied her at the waist and dragged her along with three other girls. She was made to follow them as they hunted down Philippine guerrillas. Strung together by a sturdy hemp rope, the four girls were raped every night, five times a night, a different soldier every time.

Perhaps her words are not proof enough. Then give me your hand. Sometimes when the women tell their stories and they trust that you are listening, they will guide your hands to touch their wounds. Pilar Frias has a wide flat nose and a scar that runs the length and width of it. If you run your fingers along the line of that scar, you can actually feel where the bayonet sliced her. If you run your hands along her waist, you will see the fall and rise of scars where ropes burned her skin as she was dragged through the forests with three other young women and raped each night.

Is this not evidence of coercion?

Since 1993 the women of LILA Pilipina have come forward to the dismay of their families. They have marched the streets and filed petitions to acknowledge the crimes that were placed on their bodies, on their spirits, and on the rest of their natural lives. They have traveled to Japan and appeared in your courts to tell their personal stories of sexual abuse. This is not an easy thing to do. If you understand the culture of shame that comes with such experiences, you know that their presence in this house in Quezon City, or at the gates of the Japanese embassy in Manila, or in your country's courts is evidence enough.

The women are in their eighties, and yes, they are dying. When they are gone it will be much easier to pretend that these wartime atrocities never happened. But women like Pilar Frias have many friends and supporters. We know their stories. We have touched their wounds and seen the consequences of your military's actions on their lives.

There are enough of us who know. Who are working to document their experiences. Who like them, are fighting to stop this act of violence from recurring to another daughter, to a niece, to a child.

This summer, I plan to visit the Lolas of LILA Pilipina to complete the work I've begun. Meet me there, Prime Minister Abe. Sit with us. Listen, and *then* insist you have no evidence to prove there was coercion. Unless you believe that women's lives hold no value—that the wounds that mar their bodies, that stain their minds, and have affected their lives hold no value for you.

Sincerely,
M. Evelina Galang

Lost in Translation

I COUNT SIXTEEN people who either volunteered or were paid to transcribe and translate the interviews with the lolas. Only nine of them translated anything. The others were lost when the lola spoke too fast, too soft, too deep. Lost in the mail. Lost in cyberspace. I cannot figure out what happens after they receive the material and begin. I only know that I have learned not to count on anyone anymore.

I am pleased when they offer. I exchange polite emails with them. I ask for their addresses. I transfer the VHS and high-definition tapes onto DVDs to make them easier to work with. I mail the materials. I say thank you a thousand times thank you. And then I say a prayer. I hold my breath. Transcribing is tedious work, after all, translating these stories, brutal.

So often, the lola begins facing that camera, ready and willing to tell her tale. And every time she states her name, her age, and the city of her birthplace. Then, her story. She is walking down a path, or cooking at the stove, or bathing her baby. These things she tells us in English. When suddenly, the attackers enter. Kura! Kura! She slips into Tagalog, assigns made-up words for the Japanese soldiers. And then they take her. Some can tell you in the national language, in Filipino, in Tagalog, in a steady unemotional narrative, but more often than not, the lola will slip into Visayan, Kapampangan, Ilocano, and some will speak in tribal tongue—Waray for example. Some cannot make it through without a hiccup, a pause, a sigh deep and guttural. Some will mix the languages up into a cocktail of words drowning in a sea of sadness. The crying swallows up much of the story. And then there are the moments when she reveals the scars—on the arm, or the calf, on a temple near the left eye, on the bone of her breast.

I cannot tell you why I lose the translators one by one. But I do. Sometimes they say they have other things going on. Or they tell me they have lost the DVDs. Sometimes they say nothing but simply disappear. Maybe they have fallen under the spell of the lolas' testimonies, falling asleep in libraries, at office desks, and in cafés all over Manila.

"Hindi ko kaya," says one of my nieces, pleading in an email. "Hindi na talaga kaya ng body ko, ng utak ko, auntie. Please don't make me do it."

Daughter of
This Country

December 29, 2015

"**WHO ARE YOU?**" asks an old Korean woman. "What did you do?" Her voice rises against the constant clatter of cameras popping and flashing. She holds her head up as she confronts the government official. Smiling, he extends his hand to her. She ignores it. "Why are you killing us twice?" she demands.

I'm watching a video of South Korean vice minister Lim Sung-Nam at the shelter for "comfort women" survivors in Yeonnam-dong, Seoul. It is the day after Japan and South Korea have made a joint announcement. In the video, Lim asks the old woman to sit down. She refuses. "Did you exclude us because we are uneducated—because I am too old?"

He doesn't flinch. Not even when she accuses him of being a Japanese collaborator. He never stops smiling. "I am the daughter of this country," she says. No change in Lim Sung-Nam. By the time the video is over, I realize my hands are clenched tight.

I know this old woman. She is Lee Yong-Su, one of the last of the remaining "comfort women" survivors of South Korea. The last time I saw her, we were on Capitol Hill, celebrating the passage of House Resolution 121. Unlike the vision of her today, she was light on her feet then—dancing, smiling, and singing karaoke with Congressman Mike Honda and me.

For more than twenty years, the survivors throughout Asia have been asking Japan to make a public apology, to document these atrocities of war, and to give monetary reparations for the injuries the women and their families suffered during World War II.

Japan has consistently refused their demands. The government has never apologized or paid wartime reparations. Though Chief Cabinet Secretary Yohei Kono made a personal apology in 1993, the Japanese government has never asked the women to forgive them.

On December 28, 2015, the governments of Japan and South Korea announced an end to the long-simmering dispute. In the agreement, Japanese prime minister Shinzō Abe acknowledged the suffering of the South Korean "comfort women" and made a promise of apology as well as monetary reparations. In return, South Korea recognized Japan's desire for the removal of a "comfort woman" memorial in front of the Japanese embassy. South Korea pledged to "strive to solve this issue in an appropriate manner." The agreement stipulates that the "comfort women" matter is "resolved finally and irreversibly," and that South Korea, along with Japan, will "refrain from accusing or criticizing each other regarding this issue in the international community."

Each nation made its own statement. The agreement was not officially written down; neither government voted on it. No survivors were consulted before, during, or after the agreement was made. No wonder Lee Yong-Su is so angry.

Like the 1993 Kono Statement, the recent agreement is an acknowledgment made by the Japanese prime minister, not the government. A sincere apology would not have excluded "comfort women" outside of South Korea, it would have heard the demands from all "comfort women," and it would ensure that history would never repeat itself. The Japanese would demonstrate sincerity through documentation, education, and the memorialization of its crimes against "comfort women" in international forums, textbooks, and schools. A sincere apology would not be contingent on removing statues or silencing governments.

Rather than documenting and honoring the World War II "comfort women," Japan is insisting on the removal of the memorial to survivors, as well as what amounts to a gag order on South Korea. Why? Because Japan wants to eliminate the "comfort women" from history. In December 2015, Japanese scholars protested the depiction of "comfort women" in a McGraw-Hill history textbook, objecting to, among other things, the assertion that the Japanese Army forced women into the sex-slave camps. McGraw-Hill, supported by a number of American scholars, has stood fast.

Imagine if the German government sought through diplomacy to inveigle other governments to alter textbooks, to downplay its World War II responsibilities, and to remove Holocaust memorials.

The Japanese–South Korean settlement is nothing less than an agreement to efface history by co-opting its most vigorous opponent on the "comfort women" issue. Among the nations whose women were coerced and raped during World War II, only South Korea has demanded an apology and reparations for its survivors. If South Korea agrees to stop talking about "comfort women," removes memorials and references to them, and accepts that the issue is "resolved finally and irreversibly," then what will become of survivors outside of South Korea? Is it likely that nations who have yet to step up on behalf of their daughters will do so now that the loudest voice has been silenced? I doubt it.

In Manila, the remaining Filipina "comfort women," in an attempt to get President Benigno Aquino III's attention, folded colorful origami peace cranes. Japanese Emperor Akihito and Empress Michiko were on a state visit in the Philippines from January 26 to 30, 2016. LILA Pilipina made their request known in this beautiful and symbolic gesture, and when Aquino ignored them, the lolas began speaking out, along with several hundred supporters on the streets of Manila. They wanted their president to talk to the emperor and empress about their struggle for justice. Aquino remained silent.

Over the past eighteen years, I have seen the Filipina "comfort women" demonstrating in the streets of Manila, standing up to their own government through the administrations of three sitting presidents. With each year, I have watched the women shrink with age. Each year their bodies weaken. Fewer of them remain. Their struggle has always been for the future. Not just for the Filipina "comfort women" of World War II, but all "comfort women." Not just for "comfort women," but all women of all nations.

Why? Because this issue is about the perpetual abuse of women in war—at home and abroad, between nations, among communities, and within families. This is about women and their bodies. Who has a right to them? Who protects them? Who honors them and who denies them? It is about that dignity that is torn from each girl, each woman, each nation's daughter, every time she is taken against her will, violated, and left for dead.

When I sat in Congress on July 30, 2007, and heard each representative rise to support House Resolution 121, I was filled with great pride for my country, the United States of America. As Congressman Honda said on that day, "Historical reconciliation is not just a concept to be championed, but has very real consequences in the lives of the many women institutionally victimized during World War II." Nine years later, Secretary of State John Kerry and the United States are endorsing this agreement between South Korea and Japan and I am disappointed. While former Congressman Eni F. H. Faleomavaega and Representative Mike Honda have publicly stated the flaws of this agreement, Congress should use its diplomatic influence to demand a full apology for all "comfort women," as they did when they passed House Resolution 121. The current agreement is not enough.

If I thought a woman's voice held any weight with these governments, I would ask Japan and South Korea to reassess this so-called apology. I would ask them to consider not only the 400,000 women who were kidnapped and held as military sex slaves in World War II, I would also ask them to think of their own daughters and granddaughters. In what way does your agreement honor and protect them? In what way do you demonstrate leadership and humanity to the world? In what way do you honor your mothers?

Roses

"**WHEN YOU LISTEN** to the lolas," my friend Karen tells me, "Hold a rose up between you."

"Like a microphone?" I ask.

"Like a filter."

If I think about what a lola is telling me, if I imagine the act of abduction, the sound of her voice, the weight of a soldier on her body—and not just one soldier but many—and not just one time, but repeatedly—I think I might not make it.

The fatigue takes over. My mind shuts down. I want to dwell on those moments when we are singing to ABBA's "Dancing Queen." I want to think that a dozen old women in purple T-shirts, marching in front of Malacañang Palace, might move a sitting president to speak up on their behalf, demand justice, stand up to the Japanese prime minister.

I dream of justice. I dream the lolas have stopped crying. I dream that this atrocity won't happen again—not in the Philippines, not in the United States, not in the Democratic Republic of Congo. I dream there will be justice.

And then I wake and face the dozens of tapes where I have asked the women to give their testimonies. I look onto the screen and I see the extreme close-ups of a temple, an ear, the weight of a tear trickling down a wrinkled face. If I hear her voice and imagine what she is telling me is happening right now, I feel every cell in my body perk up. I cannot sit still, even as I yawn. I cannot rest, even as I write down her words.

246

I change my screen saver. I choose an image of a thousand plucked red rose petals and I stretch the photo across the screen. Their stories push through a bed of roses, filtered, clear. It's only an image, and yet the thought of the lolas speaking into a beautiful blossom with its many layers of red velvet, gives me just enough distance. Somehow I am able to witness their lives without taking on their trauma.

I know that every time they speak their story, the moment comes alive. It is not something from the past for them, it is the real-time experience happening all over again.

When, in November 2004, I hear of the suicide of author Iris Chang, I cannot help myself. I mourn. She was a daughter of Chinese immigrants, an American writer who went abroad to document the narratives of those Chinese survivors of the Nanking Massacre for her book *The Rape of Nanking*. I can never know what happened, but I can only imagine how she felt. I know what it means to be born an American of immigrant parents, and to return to that homeland to hear the stories of wartime rape and torture on your elders, to feel the drive to right that wrong. To make a promise to see that justice done in the face of the impossible. Even if your only weapons are words, are testimonies, are stories.

I will never know what happened to her, but when I hear of Iris Chang, I grow sad and quiet. I wonder if she had a rose to hold up to her survivors. I wonder what filters there were to keep the distance of their experiences from ravaging her own body. I say a prayer for her. I light a candle. I wish her peace.

filipino "comfort women" of world war II

The following lists are based on information I received from LILA Pilipina during my Fulbright research in 2002.

A PARTIAL LIST OF SURVIVORS OF WARTIME RAPE CAMPS

The list below includes the names of the women, the site of the abduction or "comfort station," and the year they were abducted.

Flocerpida Abaño, Masbate, 1942

Francisca Acido, Manila, unknown

Maria Lourdes Alnas Acosta, Ilocos, 1943

Estela Adriatico, Manila, 1944

Emeteria Julian Adriatico, Abra 1942

Virginia Aguilar, unknown

Cristita Alcober, Leyte, 1944

Benita Aliganza, Leyte, 1944

Lucia Alvarez, Samar 1944

Juanita Antiola, unknown

Lydia Antonio, Pampanga, 1944

Emiliana Dela Cruz Aranque, Iloilo, 1944

Vitaliana Araoarao, unknown, 1942

Patrocinia Argote, unknown

Eduarda Espra Aro, Cebu, 1944

Paula Gaste Atillo, unknown

Milagros Lopez Aton, Cebu, 1943

Francisca Napiza Austari, Laguna, 1941

Gloria T. Avila, Leyte, unknown

Condrada Ayao, Bohol, 1944

Placida Balahay, Bohol, 1942

Amonita Balajadia, Isabela, 1942

Nenita Gertrude Balisalisa, Bikol, unknown

Asuncion Balmes-Adol, Bikol, 1942

Nena Balmori, Pangasinan, 1942

Victoriana Bamoya, Davao, 1941

Flora Banton, Bikol, 1943

Prescila Bartonico, Leyte, 1941

Cora Bermejo, Capiz, 1943

Saturnina Bermoy Bersano, Bohol, 1941

Crising Borga, Laguna, 1945

Francisca Borja Jose, Bohol, 1945

Anecita Medel Bravo, Negros Occidental, 1941

Isabel Asumbrado Bul-An, Agusan del Norte, 1944

Juliana Burgos, Cebu, unknown

Hilaria Bustamante, Bataan, 1943

Roberta Caballa, Cebu, 1942

Honoria Cabasag, Antique, 1943

Dionisia Monetcastro Cahulao, Negros Occidental, 1942

Fidela Carpina, Leyte, 1943

Placida Carranza, Bikol, 1944

Regina T. Cayanan, Bulacan, 1945

Purita Santos Cañedo, Manila, 1944

Betelina Bascon Cañezo, Davao, 1944

Narcisa Adriatico Claveria, Abra, 1942

Susana Condeza, Leyte, 1944

Lolita Consolacion, Pangasinan, 1942

Corazon Cornel, Iloilo, unknown

Atanacia Cortez, Manila, 1943

Roberta Lamdagan Danila, Bohol, 1942

Fedencia Nacar David, Pangasinan, 1942

Dominga De Guzman, unknown

Felicidad De Los Reyes, Masbate, 1942

Consolacion Cabrera de los Santos, Manila, 1943

Tranquilina de los Santos, Negros Occidental, unknown

Felicidad Bornalez Decandulo, Capiz, 1942

Maria Del Campo, Davao, 1944

Anita Del Mundo, Capiz, 1944

Concepcion San Andres Desillarico, Manila, 1941

Remedios Dialino, Leyte, 1944

Rosita Buella Dimas, Bikol, 1943

Lourdes Divinagarcia, Iloilo, unknown

Brigida Chavez Duaso, Bikol, 1945

Maria Duites, Bohol, 1942

Estelita Dy, Negros Occidental, unknown

Nieves Eborde, unknown

Lorenza Gella Erida, Antique, 1942

Lourdes Escober, Bikol, 1944

Lolita Felicidario Espineda, Bikol, unknown

Dominga Esponilla, Iloilo, 1943

Crisanta Estolonio, Bikol, 1943

Remedios Estorminos Felias, Leyte, 1943

Marina Empaano Feliciano, Bulacan, 1942

Andresa Fernandez, Davao, 1943

Petronila Fernandez, Pangasinan, 1944

Rufina Fernandez, Manila, unknown

Momie Fiel, Leyte, 1943

Juana Dakay Francisco, Cebu, 1944

Pilar Frias, Bikol, 1943

Wenceslawa Maceren Gaas, Bohol, unknown

Angelina Posadas Gabuya, Negros Occidental, 1944

Basilisa Ganansyal, Negros
    Occidental, unknown
Lourdes Gaspar, Capiz, unknown
Elena Chiao Gedelia, Bikol, 1945
Fe Fresnosa Hedia, Bikol, 1945
Maria Rosa Luna Henson,
    Pampanga, 1941
Rosita Herbosa, Bikol, unknown
Rufina Hernandez, Marinduque,
    1942
Felicidad Hilado, Negros
    Occidental, unknown
Gavina Bermoy Ho, Bohol, unknown
Gregoria Ibañez, Leyte, 1942
Salud Ingking, Bohol, unknown
Teodora Cogonon Intes, Negros Occi-
    dental, 1942
Juanita Jamot, Manila, 1945
Felicitas Jampolina, Bikol, 1944
Celerina Josol, Leyte, 1943
Dionisia Medalla Jumapit,
    Bataan, 1941
Alejandra Bonilla Lampitoc,
    Pangasinan, 1945
Violeta Lanzarote, Iloilo, 1942
Teresa Linguillas, Davao, unknown
Victoria Canlas Lopez, Pampanga,
    1942
Josefa Lopez Villamar, Manila, 1944
Catalina Lorenzo, Davao, 1944
Eufrocina Lorenzo, unknown
Ely Ramirez Lorenzo, Nueva Ecija,
    1942
Francisca Macabebe, Iloilo, 1942
Adelina Majuelo, Manila, 1942
Encarnacion Malicdem, Pangasinan,
    unknown
Maria Manares, Manila, 1945

Primitiva A. Mandras, Leyte, 1942
Agriana Manuel, Nueva Ecija,
    unknown
Virginia Manuel, Nueva Ecija, un-
    known
Simplicia Marilag, Manila, 1943
Ortencia Guzman Martinez,
    Masbate, 1942
Lolita Villacote Mendez, Bikol, 1943
Rebecca Tuazon Mendoza,
    Zambales, 1943
Purificacion Mercado, Bikol, 1943
Salud Miranda
Lucia Misa
Dolores Molina, Manila 1943
Rosita Nacino
Piedad Nobleza, Aklan, 1942
Rosario Nopueto
Sabina Villegas Ocampo
Lucia Opelac
Felicidad Plicar
Julia Porras
Trinidad Rabusa
Carmencita Ramel, Bulacan, 1944
Simeona Ramil
Eutiquina Rivera
Estelita Morandante Salas
Tomasa Salinog
Urduja Samonte, Aklan, 1944
Remigia Macapagal San Pedro,
    Manila 1942
Bernarda Clave Sancho, Bikol, 1942
Gertrudes Santillan, Manila, unknown
Maria Fe Santillan, unknown, 1943
Pacita Suclan Santillan, Antique,
    1943
Aurora Sarcino, Aklan, 1944
Correa Simeon, Aklan, 1943

Purificacion Sonza, Laguna 1942

Adela Sumagpang, Quezon
Province, 1945

Maria Tabia de Lima, Laguna, 1944

Remedios Francisco Tecson, 1944

Esperanza Tolosa, Negros
Occidental, 1944

Catalina Torrevillas, unknown

Marcelina Trapalgar, unknown

Demetria Tubac, Bohol, 1942

Catalina Ufalsa, Bikol, 1943

Remedios Valencia, unknown, 1942

Feliza Vallejos, Nueva Ecija,
unknown

Melicia Varde, Bikol, 1945

Dionisia Velasquez, Quezon
Province, 1945

Justina Pido Villanueva, Negros
Occidental, 1944

Virginia Villarma, Manila, 1943

Virginia Villegas, Pampanga, 1942

Leona Zafra, Cebu, 1943

PLAINTIFFS FOR POSTWAR COMPENSATION SUIT

Filed April 2, 1993

1. Maria Rosa Henson
2. Atanacia Cortez
3. Tomasa Salinog
4. Estelita Morandante Salas
5. Rosario Nopueto
6. Francisa Austari
7. Julia Porras
8. Sabina Villegas Ocampo
9. Rosita Nacino
10. Juanita Jamot
11. Maria Fe Santillan
12. Simplicia Marilag
13. Cristita Alcober
14. Justina Pido Villanueva
15. Victoria Canlas Lopez
16. Purificacion Mercado
17. Rufina Fernandez
18. Felicidad Decandulo

Filed September 1993

1. Dionisia Jumapit
2. Gertrude Balisalisa
3. Amonita Balajadia
4. Maria Manares
5. Carmencita Ramel
6. Ortencia Martinez
7. Lucia Misa
8. Fedencia David
9. Pacita Santillan
10. Pilar Frias
11. Violeta Lanzarote
12. Purita Cañedo
13. Fe Hedia
14. Felicitas Jampolina
15. Hilaria Bustamante
16. Narcisa Claveria
17. Maria del Campo
18. Andresa Fernandez
19. Remedios Valencia
20. Catalina Lorenzo
21. Lolita Felicidario Espineda
22. Condrada Ayao
23. Roberta Caballa
24. Pacida Carranza
25. Felicidad de los Reyes
26. Adelina Majuelo
27. Piedad Nobleza
28. Catalina Ufalsa

August 1996	Maria Rosa Henson	June 1998	Violeta Lanzarote
	Atanacia Cortez		Remedios Valencia
	Rufina Fernandez	July 1998	Pilar Frias
	Juanita Jamot		
September 1996	Purita Cañedo	August 1998	Dionisia Jumapit
			Ortencia Martinez
October 1996	Estelita Salas		Felicidad Decandulo
			Juliana Burgos
November 1996	Victoria Lopez		
		September 1998	Salud Miranda
December 1996	Fe Hedia		
		December 1998	Josefa Lopez
June 1997	Felicitas Jampolina		Villamar
	Lolita Espineda		Amonita Balajadia
	Rosita Nacino		Estela Adriatico
			Maria Manarez
July 1997	Dolores Molina		
	Remedios Felias	January 1999	Catalina Lorenzo
			Lucia Misa
September 1997	Maria Fe Santillan		
		February 1999	Felicidad de los
October 1997	Fedencia David		Reyes
	Cora Bermejo		Paula Atillo
	Andresa Fernandez		Prescila Bartonico
	Purificacion Mercado		Virginia Villarma
	Narcisa Claveria		
		April 1999	Lourdes Divina-
November 1997	Regina T. Cayanan		gracia
	Cristita Alcober		
		May 1999	Julia Porras
December 1997	Remedios Tecson		Benita Aliganza
January 1998	Francisca Austari	June 1999	Rosario Nopueto
	Hilaria Bustamante		
		July 1999	Francisca Macabebe
February 1998	Sabina Ocampo		
		August 1999	Carmencita Ramel
March 1998	Placida Carranza		Estelita Dy
			Remedios Dialino

September 1999	Piedad Nobleza Correa Simeon	December 2000	Catalina Torrevillas
October 1999	Lucia Alvarez	February 2001	Virginia Villegas Isabel Bul-an
	Teodora Intes Trinidad Rabusa	July 2001	Simeona Ramil Flora Banton
	Urduja Samonte Francisca Acido	August 2001	Georgia Ibañez
	Lolita Mendez	March 2002	Nieves Eborde
December 1999	Juanita Antiola		Condrada Ayao
	Petronila Fernandez		Milagros Aton
	Crisanta Estolonio		Eutiquina Rivera
	Maria Tabia de Lima		Felicidad Policar
			Justina Pido- Villanueva
January 2000	Catalina Ufalsa Flocerpida Abaño		Esperanza Tolosa
	Lucia Opelac		Anecita Medel Bravo
April 2000	Bernarda Sancho		Tranquilina de los Santos
May 2000	Emeteria Adriatico		
	Maria del Campo	May 2002	Roberta Caballa
			Pacita Santillan
July 2000	Lydia Antonio		

Monday's Luminous Mysteries

An Afterword

With the women of LILA Pilipina, 49 Matimpiin Street, May 6, 2002. Since then, Lolas' House, now Lolas' Center, has moved from Matimpiin Street to Narra Street in the baranggay of Amihan, Quezon City, Metro Manila.

Mga Lola,

ABBA's song, "Dancing Queen," reverberates throughout my galley
kitchen. Do you remember this song, our song? The one that got
every one of you up and out of the plastic chairs at Lolas' House? All
the little lolas, boogieing to the beat of 1970s disco? Today, I move to
that beat, rolling out dough for pan de coco, shaping it into perfect
circles. The filling, a mixture of coconut and condensed milk, sits in
the center of each pocket of dough. The seams are pulled together
and set with a paintbrush of egg wash.

Next, the sinigang. Because this is Miami, where there are no milk
fish, instead of bangus, I use salmon. Chunks of tomatoes, quartered
onions, and sliced ginger swirl to a boil in a tamarind-seasoned base.
The white rice steams on the stove, sending a beautiful scent of jas-
mine into the air.

I plate the food on miniature saucers, pour isang tasa ng kape,
instant with lots of sugar and milk. Orange Royal soda fizzes into a
cold shot glass.

During our time together, these were the foods you offered me
whenever I came to your homes.

Underneath the banana leaves, a beautiful woven mat from Kalibo
spreads before the feet of Mama Mary. A small dark figure, a woman carved of Philippine wood, sits cross-legged next to the Virgin.
On the batik, the miniature plates of food float like seven thousand
islands in the South Seas.

In an envelope marked "Apology" I leave a love letter, a sorry note,
a personal wish that you receive all the things you are asking for and
an apology for my inability to make things happen quicker for you. A
one-hundred-peso note peeks from behind a DVD of Lolas' House. An
intricately carved wooden fan spreads like butterfly wings.

I bow my head, think of all of you—you who are still marching on
the streets, you who are on your sick beds and dying, you who have

moved on and into the spirit world. I see your faces. Your thin arms. Your not-so-steady gait. I hear your voices. In my memory you are beautiful but aging faster than the sun crossing western skies. You have been so brave. You have been stronger than any of your supporters. You get up, you fight. Until your last breath, you fight.

Last January, when I was teaching at the NVM Gonzales Writing Workshop, I took a ferry to Mindanao and one of my students told me about making offerings to the ancestors. She was looking for guidance.

"What do you offer them?" I asked.

"Whatever I think they want," she answered.

I knew this was what I had to do. I had to come back to Miami and begin making offerings to all of you. I had to pray for guidance. And so every Monday, I pray the Luminous Mysteries. I love the third mystery that says, "Blessed are they who hunger and thirst for justice, for they shall be satisfied."

I meditate on these things. I talk to all of you. I ask for guidance. I ask you how you want your stories told. I say, "Kamusta kayo?"

Soon after I begin praying these Luminous Mysteries, I receive an email from Lola Dolor's grandson, Carl Lewis Molina, a boy who has never written me before. He is now a young man in Manila who has continued his grandmother's campaign for justice.

The last time we were together, Lola Dolor, you wondered how I would know when you were gone. You said that if I was in America and I felt the wind brush my skin, I would know. I laughed at you, and I said that if that happened, it meant Dolor was there. And now, the trees are dancing in a rush of Miami wind. Your grandson wrote me, just as I was wondering about all of you. When I told Carl this story, he wrote back:

"Thank you so much! I really enjoyed reading your story. I was also glad to know that you and my lola are close friends. I know that she's very happy right now, knowing that you [are] still fighting and praying for them, for the lolas.

"Lola Dolor died last June 3, 2009. She [is] buried at the Manila North Cemetery. Our family didn't have enough money to give her a proper burial service, she doesn't even have a gravestone. But

I promised my Lola that someday I will transfer her remains in a proper tomb and the justice that she always wanted will be served properly."

On the one hand, I am delighted to hear from your grandson, Lola Dolor. But to hear that you were not able to receive a proper burial breaks my heart. And that is why the fight continues.

Today, I offer all the women of Lolas' House this book. I thank you for your constant struggle for justice. I thank you for showing us how to speak your truth without hesitation. I have been honored to sit in your presence, mga lola. On this day, 1 July 2017, there is still no formal apology from the Japanese government. Your friends and family are still fighting. Me too. If anything changes, I will let you know.

In love and solidarity,
Evelina

ACKNOWLEDGMENTS

Lolas' House is a book of protest, impossible to produce without my community of activists. Mostly women, they introduced me to the lolas, led me deep into my research, helped me interview, transcribe, translate. Some stood with me on the steps of the Japanese embassy, the U.S. embassy, and Malacañang Palace.

My most sincere thanks to Rechilda Extremadura, Ninotchka Rosca, Liza Maza, Nelia Sancho, Pearl Ubugen, Sol Rapisura, Arcelita Imasa, Vim Nadera, and Sister Mary John Mananzan for making it possible for me to know the lolas.

To the dalagas who have journeyed with me all these years in miles, in spirit, and in friendship—Ana Fe Muñoz, Tara Agtarap, Nelhe Bacarse Poletsky, Mia Habon, and Lizzie Juaniza, Shin Yu Pai, and Luba Winship. And to my former business partner, Hugh Haller, who helped finance the Dalaga Project. Thanks.

In gratitude to the Fulbright Scholar Program, the Fulbright Philippine-American Education Foundation, and the University of Miami for funding *Lolas' House* research and travel. Salamat sa University of the Philippines Creative Writing for hosting me.

Thank you to the editors of the anthologies *All That Glitters*, *Kartika Review*, and *Hanggan sa Muli* for including portions of this work in their publications.

To Faustino Bong Cardiño—maraming salamat. You not only drove me and the lolas to the places we needed to go to, but you became our friend, and in doing so, a warrior for justice, too.

To those who have transcribed, translated, copyedited, and transferred the interviews for *Lolas' House*. Maraming salamat, Leah Silvieus, Michelle Ayroso, Cindy Ayroso Reyes, Carmen Ayroso, Betina De Borja Relator, Rubee Gugol Galang, Ysabel Zuniga-Palileo, Jillian Temblique-Rosal, Carl Benedict Cruz, Jenicka Hosaka, Ava Hanlyn, Kirsten Quito-Bausa, John Co, Nina Lagac, Jeanna Hamilton, and Kat Cruz.

To my community of activists for your constant support and your fight for justice in the name of the lolas. For your support of House Resolution 121, the "Comfort Women" resolution, thank you Rita Wong, Carole Villamaria, Gayle Mendoza, Elaine Tuner Lee, Amberly Reynolds, Cyd Apellido, M. G. Bertulfo, and Theresa de Leon Jaranilla. Thank you, Annabel Park and Eric Byler. For your leadership and for taking H.Res.121 out of markup and to the House of Representatives, I am grateful to the late congressman Tom Lantos, grateful to Mike Honda, Ileana Ros-Lehtinin, and Nancy Pelosi. Thank you to my Filipino American network of leaders and educators—to Marily Mondejar, Bing Cardenas Branigin, Ben de Guzman, Jon Melegrito, Joy Bruce, Allyson Tintiangco-Cubales, and Dawn Bohulano Mabalon. Super salamat, comares at compadres.

To an amazing support team at Curbstone Books led by Gianna Francesca Mosser, and to everyone connected to the production of this book, including Nívea Castro, Morgan H. McKie, and Michelle Blankenship. Thank you.

Writing in a community of strong women has supported me through all drafts, notes, and revisions of this book. To my sisters Elmaz Abinader, Lara Stapleton, Deb Busman, Gina Apostol, Maureen Seaton, Cristina Garcia, Faith Adiele, and Edwidge Danticat. To my heroine Maxine Hong Kingston—you have shown me the way and I am so thankful. To Johanna Poethig—you took the lolas' stories and shared them with a wide and beautiful tribe of artists and performers and now *Lolas' House* has a companion in *Songs for Women Living with War*. You, too, are fighting for justice and I am grateful to you.

To my family and the many ways you have supported the writing of this book. Thank you Uncle Romeo Lopez-Tan and Anna Karina Bate Lopez-Tan for your support in the Philippines. Thank you, Auntie Dolores T. Galang, for filling in the blanks. To my parents, Miguel and Gloria Galang, to my siblings, to my nephews and nieces, and to my stepdaughters, son-in-law, and grandson, Jaiden Carlos Vazquez. Here's hoping the lolas' dream comes true: Never again.

To my love, my husband, Chauncey Mabe. Lola Josefa got it right. I got only one husband, you. Your support is magnificent beyond words.

In solidarity and gratitude to the organizations of GABRIELA, LILA Pilipina, and GABRIELA Network, for your continual support and help in organizing the research, travel, and multiple interviews with the lolas and their pamiliya. Maraming salamat sa inyong lahat.

And to the sixteen lolas who have opened up and shared their testimonies with me over and over again, maraming salamat, po. To you Catalina Lorenzo, Virginia Villarma, Lucia Alvarez, Pilar Frias, Benita Aliganza, Cristita Alcober, Narcisa Adriatico Claveria, Violeta Lanzarote, Prescila Bartonico, Dolores Molina, Piedad Nicasio Nobleza, Josefa Lopez Villamar, Atanacia Cortez, Urduja Francisco Samonte, Carmencita Cosio Ramel, and Remedios Felias. Mano, po. I am honored to have known you. Wherever you are, I hope you find peace. I hope you find justice. I hope you know that I will never rest until it comes. Laban! Laban! Laban!

400,000

IN MARCH 2016, I took the stage with four other scholars, journalists, and activists. The conference, "Unfinished Apologies: Imperial Japan's Sex Slaves of Wartime Asia," organized by Asia Point Policy and John Hopkins University, was the first time I had been among other women who had been researching "comfort women" of World War II. The women's work involved survivors from Japan, Korea, Indonesia, and the Dutch East and West Indies. I shared my research from this book.

For years, historians have been telling us that 200,000 women and girls were abducted and made to serve in military sex-slave camps by the Imperial Japanese Army. Dr. PeiPei Qui revealed that an additional 200,000 Chinese "comfort women" had been left out of those initial numbers. The tally is closer to 400,000.

Coming together to deliver our findings, we found a sisterhood among us, a conviction to unearth these unspoken stories and document them. We found that we shared the same fire for justice.

The fight for all "comfort women" continues. The Japanese government refuses to recognize the 400,000 women and girls, refuses to offer a formal apology, reparations and documentation in their historical texts. And so we write.

I am honored to have presented with Hilde Janssen, Griselda Molemans, Caroline Norma, and Peipei Qiu, women warriors who have contributed to this growing body of work.

FURTHER READING

Banning, Jan, and Hilde Janssen. *Troostmeisjes/Comfort Women*. Utrecht: Banning, 2013.

Felias, Remedios. *The Hidden Battle of Leyte: The Picture Diary of a Girl Taken by the Japanese Miliary*. Tokyo: Bucung Bucong, 1998.

Henson, Maria Rosa. *Comfort Woman: Slave of Destiny*. Pasig City, Metro Manila: Philippine Center for Investigative Journalism, 1996.

Molemans, Griselda. *A Lifetime of War*. Forthcoming, 2017.

Norma, Caroline. *The Japanese Comfort Women and Sexual Slavery during the China and Pacific Wars*. New York: Bloomsbury Academic, 2015.

Qiu, PeiPei. *Chinese Comfort Women: Testimonies from Imperial Japan's Sex Slaves*. New York: Oxford University Press, 2013.

Sancho, Nelia. *War Crimes on Asian Women*. Manila: Asian Women Human Rights Council, 1998.

Stez, Margaret, and Bonnie B. C. Oh. *Legacies of the Comfort Women of World War II*. London and New York: Routledge, 2001.

Washington Coalition for Comfort Women Issues. *Comfort Women's Testimony of Military Sexual Slavery by Japan*. McLean Va.: Washington Coalition for Comfort Women Issues.

Women's International Day
March 7, 2002